To

King S[...]

best of luck skipper

14th 10th 1993

POETRY NOW

MATING RITUALS

1993

Edited by Veronica Hannon

First published in Great Britain in 1993 by
POETRY NOW
1-2 Wainman Road, Woodston,
Peterborough, PE2 7BU

All Rights Reserved

Copyright Contributors 1993

FOREWORD

I remember one evening, after being to see a show, confiding in my mother that I was in love. I had fallen for the leading man in *Joseph and His Technicolor Dreamcoat*. Once I had broached this subject the tears began to fall as I confided that this love was totally unrequited. I had spent the show staring open mouthed at the stage and he hadn't looked at me once!

Years later over coffee my mother related this story to me. She revealed that she had had difficulty in keeping a straight face at my emotional dilemma, but in her voice was a touch of concern that I had started down the road of passion so early on in life - as I was only five and the leading man was seven.

I suppose one of the things that this book illustrates is that we've all had incidents like this many times during our lives. The search for our perfect partner can cause us to go to what can seem - in hindsight - like the most extreme and sometimes embarrassing lengths. As we flutter our eyelashes and puff out our chests in an attempt to catch the eye of the person we desire, this can often hide a more basic and heartfelt longing.

Whilst reading and selecting the poems for this collection there were numerous times that I laughed or moaned in recognition.

Love is one of the all enduring themes but the poets in this book all add a fresh twist. Whether the saga is that of the Gold Blend Adverts or of one night stands, there is always a hint of humour or a telling insight which makes this book a compulsive read.

The poets in this anthology come from all over the country and from all walks of life. What unites them is that they have all suffered the hardships of the mating ritual and survived to tell the tale . . . and they tell it well. Whether writing in blank verse or carefully constructed rhyme, with sparkling wit or with cruel perception, the poems between these covers will strike a telling chord with everyone.

Veronica Hannon

Contents

Title	Author	Page
Camouflage	Tommy	1
The Mating Game	Marc Burrows	2
Fatal Erection or Scottish Dracula	Barbara Green	3
Waking Dream	Gary Michael Studley	5
A Removal of Self	Samantha Olson	6
Magnet	Richard Cook	7
Old Love	Ian Russell	8
Give and Take	Melissa M Terras	9
Kiss	Ian Mortimer	10
For Naleni	A K H Pang	11
Deep in my Eyes	Liz Morris	12
Convalescent	Christopher Morgan	13
Soul Mate	Kasayan	15
Flirtation Waltz	Mavis Fox	16
Fusion	Jason King	17
Spellbound	Dave Lunn	18
Michael and my Cycle	Sue Johns	19
The Stockbroker and Acanthis	Melissa Kite	20
Equinox (or . . . and so Winter Passes)	Vanessa Richards	21
Malespeak	Alison Hill	22
Marriages are not Made in Reading	Patric Cunnane	23
My Wife is a Wonderful Woman	Kevin E Sims	24
Kiss	Julie Howard	25
About Things	Ryan Gilbey	26
Untitled	Catharine A Benson	27
She Said She Would	Felix Dovell	28
The Gift of Tongues	Antony Nicholls	29
Game of Eyes	Allistair Wilson	30
Your One Night Stand	Alastair S Macmillan	31
Sky-Blue Bedhead	Ian Smith	32
In Mute Surrender	Stuart Elden	33

Saturday Night(Mare)	Jon Meehan	34
Rejection	William Barklam	35
Soldierboy	Ann Twenty Seven	36
In the Pub	Paul Joseph Thompson	38
No Automated Affair	Sean Isaac Ramnarine	39
Cornish Memoirs	Martin James Patrick D'Evelin	40
Sunday Offensive	Eleanor Dare	41
The Woman in my Room	Freddy Macha	42
Thunder and Lightning	David Ryan	43
Apple Bobbing	Emma Greengrass	45
The Silence	Grant Alan Wickman	47
Seduction	Anthony Knight	48
Your Ghost	Jessie Gordon	49
Untitled	Chris Ridgway	50
Tour of Beauty	Terry Egan	51
High Society Call-Girl	Jelly Bean Gold	52
Two Species	James W Harper	53
Adult Games	Tim Dowley	54
The Morning After the (One) Night (Stand) Before	Ruby Alexander	55
One Enchanted Evening	Tontschy Gerig	56
The Experience of Love	John Baker	57
A Happy Man	Nicholas Redfearn	58
Satyr	Mercedes	59
Thoughts	Rob Williams	60
Liaisons	Marcus McKee	61
Wasted Gifts, Love's Overflow	John Scopes	62
Initial Glimpse	Helen J Macnaughtan	63
Untitled	Hilire	64
Untitled	Martin Wheeler	65
Again	Martin A Swain	66
Bourgeois Sex	Herb Richard	67
Unspoken	Jill Dawson	68
Nature's Lovers	Juliet Cooper	69
Swallow Love	Kerry Shale	70
Among my Corots	David Rose	71

Title	Author	Page
Kissing Through a Pain of Glass	Peter Michael Rosenberg	73
Meanwhile, Upstairs at the Party	Fizz Fieldgrass	74
Unmarried Birth	Nik Hussey	75
Old Hand - New Boy	Eden Louise Mulliner	76
Caller	Tracey Beth	77
Man Menu	Sacha Colgate	78
Croydon Sandstorm	David R Morgan	79
Untitled	Ian Mole	80
Calling	Steve Verrall	81
Divinations	Sue Hubbard	82
Three O'Clock in the Morning	Lisa Bush	83
Dance Around me	Beverly J Kemp	84
One Night Stand	Jason Raper	85
Cruise Bar	Sue Bowley	86
My Bath Ran Away With a Gurgle	T J Carpenter	87
Dancing Days	John Steer	88
Coming of Age	David Read	89
At Browns Just for Fun	Ernst Schlögelhofer	90
RSVP 2020 AD	Hazel Lezah	91
Untitled	Ryeli Thomas	92
The Guide to Love Technique	Gary Marks	93
Bath Time	Paul Richards	94
Mr Heppenstall - Optician	Nick Woodall	96
Mr B. Astard	Denise O'Kelly	97
Doggerel Fashion	George M Frew	99
Shoulder Ride	Myk Johnson	100
Untitled	Kim Farley	101
Free	Katherine Gallagher	102
Johnny	Rochelle Levy	103
Love in Bloom	Ruby Anderson	104
The Quirks of Human Nature	Karen Simpson-harris	105
In my Lovers Bed, Arising	V N Jacobs	107
Louise Loves Melting Candles	Hamish Gane	108
Space Shag	Zinc Oberon	109

Title	Author	Page
The Erotic Journey	Peter Maguire	110
The Wounded Soldier	Joan Richardson	111
Self-Portrait	Susanna Roxman	112
Foreplay	Tom Miller	113
Hip Tips for Hot Dates	Glenda Richards	115
Stay for the Ride	Mireille Chan	116
Untitled	Christian de Nimes	117
Fever Pitch	Rachel Bourne	118
A Man Stood in Front of His House With Rain Descending	Ed Prichard	119
The Sprialling of Winter Ghosts	David Foster	120
Spermicidal Maniacs	King Brian Boru	121
Loving or Loved	Belinda Baily	122
The Smoke Tower	Kate Lewis	123
I See a Future you See a Candle	Todd Mortensen	124
Woman	Sean Cadwallander	125
Going Down	Rael	126
West Bay Love Song	Maureen Roberts	127
Being Celibate	John Deverson	129
Militant	Claire Newbury	130
Covetousness	Jennifer Chamberlain	131
Prey	Jacqueline M Rice	132
Song of Sharon	Rosemary Fisher	133
The Drought Club	Emma Foulger	134
Thief	Yvette Peden	135
You and me?	Ida Belso	136
Strength Will Prevail	Tessa Mondesir	137
From Smile to Satisfaction	Linda J Romain	139
In Winter	Vincent Woodcock	140
A Glance to Love	Carol Clegg	141
NB	Aidan Baker	142
Wet Dream	Pascale Presumey	143
Kodak	S Dass	144
From a Princess to Her King	Honor Crellin	145
Disciple	Felicity Napier	146

Title	Author	Page
In the Secret Garden of my Heart	Michael A Hurd	147
Maximes	Paula Brown	148
Combing	Linda E A Hudson-Cooper	149
When Men Love	Barbara Goode	150
What Durham Should Have Thought	Andy Goldie	151
Thieves	David Whatley	152
American in London	Mark Tracey Dearan	153
Sonnet	Lucy Wallace	154
Trojan?	Helen Dunton	155
Just so Susie	Tony Maude	156
No Answers No Lies	Meryl O'Rourke	157
Party Victims	Virley Trezise	158
No Impediment	Caro Manning Jeffrey	159
Meat Market Mating	Constance Jeffrey	160
The Love Game	John Gregory	161
Culmination	Eileen O'Donovan	162
Chopping Myself up	Petra Fried	163
Green Fingers	Lindsay Maynes	164
A Love Match	Barbara Courtenay	165
Snakes and Ladders	Lloyd William Whicker	166

Camouflage

In London I'm anonymous:
could shag a hippopotamus;
felate a rhinoceros,
no one would throw a fit,

but when I'm back in Peterborough,
(where the hell is Peterborough?),
old ladies scream with horror
when I suck a young tart's tit.

Tommy

The Mating Game

A passing glance, a look of desire
        Fingers twitching, palms perspire.
Looking back . . .
            Then back again,
Coyness, full of grace,
        Heart beating, be still the pain
Beat at a steady pace.

A purposeful stance, now face-to-face
Pupils dilated, desire enhanced
        Names exchanged, dialogue takes place.
Legs a-shuffling, arms like springs
        The history of lives commence.
Time passes, the nightingale sings
        Daylight, has gone hence.

A stroll by the river, arms entwined
        Calmness, fills the air.
Touching,
        Caressing,
             Kisses like wine
The start of a love affair?
Locked in passion, heavy sighs
        Dreams are made of this
Lying spent, beneath the skies
        Limp,
            Exhausted
                Languished.

A few meagre words . . .
        Insincere, inane.
Eyes eluding contact
        The motion of life, remains the same
When we play, the mating game.

Marc Burrows

Fatal Erection or Scottish Dracula

(To George)

His body was white, like the driven snow
With nipples like rosebuds all in a row,
His hair was as red as the beat of my heart
And his cock pierced me through like Cupid's fierce dart.

His body was white, like a pint of new milk
His skin was as smooth as a bale of pure silk,
He cried 'Och aye the noo!' as the Scotch sperrums gushed forth
And turned me from virgin to the witch of the North.

He fucked me to frenzy and told me rosy red lies
And proudly displayed his pink pretty prize
While his burning white body glowed with sweat and fire
As he drained my life's blood with his vampire's desire.

His hair was as red as the flames out of hell
I was scorched all to ashes and left just a shell
By his slug sleek white body that sucked out my life
And the vows on the ley lines that made me his wife.

He was whiter than Persil but as black as the night
As black as a Zulu, a soul without sight
As dark as the devil and evil as sin
As a whited sepulchre that was empty within. (Matthew 23 v 27)

He was a wax image that melted on touch
As he spoke in strange tongues of Scotch double Dutch
As I lay in his arms consumed in white fire
And gave myself up to the Scottish vampire.

For our sins were a scarlet and crimson as red
As we lay in love's furnace in my wee lonely bed
Then he ripped out my heart to the god of his pride
And left me bled white, the Scotch Dracula's bride. (Isaiah 1 v 18)

Barbara Green

Waking Dream

I saw you in a stream
My waking dream -
No canal or pool
Jammed or rusted,
Clear of eye stinging
High nosing chlorine.
Just you - in a stream
Face up - off pointing
    Water
    Lapping
    Your fresh cream back
    In supplety,
    Waving your hips
    Towards me
    On rings running from you
    To the edge.
    To my feet,
    Arched spine away
    Arms slow beating
    Stilling time
    for me again.
As ever, always,
My waking dream.

Gary Michael Studley

A Removal of Self

You turn and dance and star before me,
Establishing yourself;
producing sucking tentacle of seduction.
Screaming and laughing - an endless
      red wine stream,
Clambers through every orifice,
to cling and devour a fragile being.

Happiness is fleeting - a flash of an eye
Somewhat small scratch on
Histories vast surface.
Meaningless to the majority of humanity
Endlessly enormous to me -
      who cared too much
You cared for too little.

Demoralising touches of reconciliation.
Pushed and wilted,
      cut grass rejected from its roots.

To visit eternity and float
aimlessly for a lifetime,
deluding myself that forever is forever.
But realising deep under my fortressed
      skin
Forever is a fantasy produced and
      encouraged by poets.

Bitterness courses through veins
previously warm.
Generating a stranger with new ideals,
More tailored to a vacuum scream.

Samantha Olson

Magnet

    This is high summer: new
Golden peaks of daylight dawning,
        Sunspoilt fruit, eye gazing into eye.

    There will be riches upon the lawns:
The tomato of tulips, the half-moon receding,
        The buzz, buzz, buzz in the vines.

    Slowly you cross towards me
Like a bee to a flower, willing
        A clear causeway, blue

    As the moon-pull, with power
Beneath the soil distilling
        A dazzle like open ocean over the dew.

    What love, like water, always finds
Its true level; that brimming
        Of complete peace that mends?

    Only invincible attractions take their place
On earth as objects do, redeeming
        The silence of masks, the eyes in the trees.

Richard Cook

Old Love

I wonder if
I will make love
When I'm seventy
My back will be bent
My pencil spent
And rheumatism
All over me.

I wonder will my wife
Still love me dearly
Though no matter how loud I shout
The deaf cow probably won't hear me

If I bring home flowers
To my crinkled old girl
Will the smile in her face
Still bring joy
To my world

Will we still fight
Over sheets
On our bed
Will she ignore me
Over something I've said

Oh my love
My true love
Love that cannot be sold
Will I be in love
when I am old

Ian Russell

Give and Take

A reached for hand slips into mine -
No, I am grasped by you;
the mutual domination, submission
of intertwined fingers, emotions.

Melissa M Terras

Kiss

Our mouths are wounds. Long ago
our bodies were one pure form
and we spoke, needing no sound.

Then our mouths were torn apart.
Bloody, the frayed flesh healed.
The scars became our lips.

So now our mouths run softly
over and over each other, searching
for the way we were together

and trying to soothe our pain
we felt between us long ago
and still quietly remember.

Ian Mortimer

For Naleni

Stockings, suspenders, soft lace bra
All of these things make you my star
Cool to the touch, warm to the eye
Watching you undressing
(Oh, my, my . . .)

Feeling you close and writhing beneath me
Making me shiver, at the things that you show me
Coming so close that I hear you cry
Not from sadness or sorrow
(But oh, my, my . . .)

A K H Pang

Deep in my Eyes

What are you searching for?
    You know who I am, and what I am.
Yet you still look deep inside.
    It's as if you were missing something,
As if I hid something from you.
    Or perhaps you find me,
And the love you hold for me,
    Deep in my eyes.

Your looks of longing are not just
    aimed at me - but in me.
They have a content,
    An unrecognisable content,
But one crammed with clues.

Through your eyes you yearn,
    To learn more about me.
To sense my loneliness,
    To understand and ease my pain,
And perhaps,
    Recognise the extent of the
Love in my heart.

The latter, I believe can truly be
    Read in my eyes.
Love is not something which can
    Be hidden easily, and when found,
Hard to disguise.

You know me.
    And my love for you,
Then tell me what you see,
    Deep in my eyes.

Liz Morris

Convalescent

Not sure it isn't a dream until
the cold draught brushes
my sleep-musty skin

I dare not stir
as you walk across the room
and open the shutters

How did you get in?

Even words
have lost their shape
after all this time
so that the ones you say
ring senselessly
in my ears

And I cannot reply

You guide me to the window
and when my eyes adjust
to the leaden light

All I make out
is drizzle grey

Your parting words filter
through the muddy silence
but I turn too late:

You are gone

And now as I lie awake
and memories and pain and colours return,

**The room seems too big
without you**

Christopher Morgan

Soul Mate

The hand of fate began to write a new
chapter in my life. It told about the
words that flowed between us.
Of how our friendship grew,
And I became a part of you:

Then, as the hand faltered, the wheel
of fate began to spin. To decree a
meeting of two souls, each yearning
for a pathway,
to a clearer understanding with another.
And you became my lover:

Vibrations flowed as we formed our
affinity. Like two nuclei fusing, we
became one and larger in our loving.
All mankind we embraced as we first kissed:

Skies of blue became the book's cover,
whilst the white rolling clouds took on
the pages of my life. The sun shone brightly
melting,
The fine blanket of winter's snow.
And so our love began to grow:

Thus, the point of oblivion reached, a
timeless void. Merging, we rock in a cradle
of metaphysical slumber. I feel that I
have known you long.
Our genetic pathways wind,
For we are two of a kind:

Kasayan

Flirtation Waltz

Two pretty young girls
are very excited.
There's to be a dance,
and they've been invited.
The discussions begin.
There's a new man in town!
Will you wear your blue?
Shall I wear my hair down?
The dance has begun,
the girls sit by the wall,
seeking the stranger,
handsome and tall.
Both looking their best,
they have taken much care.
Nail varnish, make-up,
highlights in their hair.
Oh look! there he is!
Oh, he's not very tall,
in fact he's not even
good looking at all.
They thought he was going
to be perfection,
but he's rather pale,
with a spotty complexion!
He swaggers across,
his hair slicked with grease,
'Er, ya wanna dance?'
'Yes, oh yes please!'

Mavis Fox

Fusion

It's not just for the taste, of our animal musk,
It's not just our sex, not only our love,
It's not just the physical, not only the mind,
It's not the passion of frenzied grind.
What it is? I cannot show,
For words can't express, what the physical does not know,
It's a state of being, akin to the moon and sea,
It's the flame of the fire, it's you and it's me,
It's a blossom gently falling, from heaven to earth,
It's an embrace, a tear, baby's cry at birth.
It's a wind torn rain, that stings the face,
It's the pounding sea, a lone stallions grace,
It's an unused pillow in a bed that should be shared.
It's that feeling we get when our loved one's not there.
It's the gap that is filled when a partner is found,
If the right notes we share then a chord will sound.
It's our individual colours, individual tones that we bear,
And when we melt together, these colours we share.
We paint our pictures, when we dip our brush,
Different tones we merge within physical love.
It's the infinite light, it's the darkness of the void,
It's the lovers embrace, between a girl and her boy,
It's the black and the white, and their sex that's grey,
It's the stillness of the night, intruding on the dawn of each day.
It's the merging and melting, of yin within yang,
It's the spiritual bond that draws both woman and man.

Jason King

Spellbound

With her orgasm eyes and her Linda Lovelace lips
She goes like the clappers with her rubber gear and whips
Eyes are spellbound by her hypnotic hips
Men turn to mice as she fumbles with their zips

She gives a seductive wave with her tormenting tongue
She likes to trick and tease, it's her idea of fun
Are we pleased to see her or is it just a gun
If you invite her home for coffee you can guarantee she'll come!

She gets what she wants, and wants what she gets
She really goes ad lib, no need to follow text
Holding men to ransom inside her silouhette
She is armed to the teeth, her weapon is her *Sex*.

Dave Lunn

Michael and my Cycle

Michael, oh Michael come ride my cycle
My twenty eight days with your twenty one lays
Your masculine calling justifies all your balling
Female orgasm's really a maze

Michael, oh Michael come discuss this
But it's fine if you haven't the time
Ask your mates in the urinals, having a piss
Er, any idea what a clitoris is?

Michael you encourage female abstention
You and all your demands
With all your play on penetration
You shun me in my menstruation

But my blood is on your hands

Sue Johns

The Stockbroker and Acanthis

She had a thing about him.
Yawning through Sloane Square Stories she
stumbled on his pinstriped passion.

In prickly cornfields they kissed
and talked of bonds -
the stockbroker and Acanthis, reclining
on a bed of straw. Freshly cut,
it scratched her legs and gave her fits
of sneezing.

One August evening, with a clotted sky,
he thought he'd brought the blood blushing
through her paper skin
and the shock of breath which sent her flying
through apologies.

One August evening streaked with light
and lines of abandon,
the stubbled crop rubbed blotches which set
redder even than the sun.

Still, no harm done.
He irons the crease back into his trousers
and the steam wanes to a sigh of whitened breath.

Melissa Kite

Equinox (or . . . and so Winter Passes)

I know
Long arms
Wrapped around me
In the stillness
Of March at night,
While Spring readies herself
Quietly and with intent
To welcome daybreak.
The softest green,
the newest life
Commandeering through her
Wintered branches.
Death and Life struggling
Upon the breath,
The branch
Between the lips
Of sleeping lovers.
Lovers who lay bare,
Face to face,
so like Spring
And her Morning.

Vanessa Richards

Malespeak

Together, for now, but whenever the time is right
we will part; after all, forever is a long time . . .
Self-preservation is the name of the game:
don't expect too much and you won't get hurt.
(Men seemingly do not feel pain - just inflict it.)

Sleepless nights and tortured minds are, in fact,
a woman's prerogative, and should stay that way.
For men need clear heads in order to carry on ruling
the world their way - that's their prerogative.

Don't worry, there's still today, tomorrow and maybe
next week, but I never said we'd last forever, did I?
Be strong, that's what I find attractive in you and
that's what I need you to be, for my sake - do it for me.

So, let's just go with the flow and see what happens . . .
maybe we'll travel one day, see the world together.
Anyway, that's enough talking for one day, now it's time
for - Match of the Day - Yes, it's a goal!
(Whose game, whose rules, whose judgement - who cares?)

Alison Hill

Marriages are not Made in Reading

After-hours hotel encounter
She unzips her minidress
Wriggles free her shoulder
He slips night-caps from the minibar
Executive sex relieving stress

She's a power babe
Needs a man to scratch an itch
He's an engineering rep
      based near Bromwich
Their libidos twinkled in the bar
From G& T's to bedroom-
      not so very far

Now it's post-coital dawn
Sierras slumber
      by the hotel lawn
She identifies hers through net
Lined up with the lease-hire set

Early breakfast from the buffet cart
A peck, a handshake
Fix lipstick, then part

She puts her car in gear
      heads out for Reading
He phones a firm in Swindon
The maid folds away the bedding.

Patric Cunnane

My Wife is a Wonderful Woman

(with sincere apologies to anyone who does stutter, but this poem was inspired by my gorgeous wife *Betty* and Ronnie Barker's brilliant portrayal of 'Arkwright' in 'Open All Hours')

My wife is a w . . . wonderful woman
She is bonny and b . . . buxom as well
If I showed to you -
A photo or two
You'd as likely f . . . fancy her, I can tell.

She is generous with her p . . . portions
With her loving as well as her f . . . food.
If you sampled her home c . . . cooking -
Like I am fortunate enough to d . . . do
You would chuck out the Chef from the R . . . Ritzy
And get rid forever of that C . . . Cordon Bleu.

She is the f . . . finest lass in all the world
She is a p . . . pearl of great p . . . price.
My advice to young Arkwright
Who is a grabber and 'Open All Hours'
Is to ch . . . chuck out G . . . Gladys Emmanuel
And chat up a woman like my B.Bare . . . Betty -
Because he'd get in a stew over her dumplings
And f . . . fall for her Basmati Rice.

Kevin E Sims

Kiss

We look at the ceiling together
Afraid
to look at the bed
Your foot entwines with mine
across my face spreads
a glorious smile
I take a deep breath
and you say
would you like a cigarette?
not yet
So we drink coffee quietly
touch accidentally
I laugh behind my hair
because you amaze me.
then you kiss me
swoop in and kiss me
kiss me for so long
then you break away
manly
Smile like a boy
and I want to cry
because I found you.

Julie Howard

About Things

They were thought
to be a couple. Two cars
slept in the driveway.
Before noon she brushed

slushed crab-apples from
the path. On Sundays
there was dancing in the
upstairs window. Summer

saw them home at twilight
with bags of goldfish struck
from hoopla stalls and
nuggets of sand and seasalt

powdered undernail. They
gathered shells. He made
a necklace.
It had brittle music.

When she could not rise
he fetched the milk in bare legs
and buttocks. There were
no guests not ever.

In fact everyone was wrong.
She was teaching him about
things. Now he's taught
and she's gone.

Ryan Gilbey

Untitled

Once when they came here, aflame here, with shame here,
the joy in their bodies was full in their minds.

Now that their dreams are dead, emptiness fills their heads,
no passion now instead, love's left behind.

Maybe they always knew, still now in what they do
echo emotions they so hoped to find -

but where their feelings go, they know they'll never know.
Now all they care is how each is unkind.

Catharine A Benson

She Said She Would

Not much to tell,
Not much to say,
Story's the same,
Same as yesterday.

Baby didn't phone,
She didn't call,
Well that's not friendly,
Not friendly at all!

Felix Dovell

The Gift of Tongues

entails talent, but without elites.
The alertly versatile's loose heart,
limber from first suckling to the last
syllable, still seldom, reflexes

sharp or controlled saintly, this organ
can be quaver small and then as long
as a whole corpus of overtures.
Most work normally undercover,

a lisp or fat sloth though will evoke
constantly. Hard kissing brings closest
its secular urge, the embroiling

of equal muscular dumb passion.
Potently harmless, its keen caress
clean whisks in all-round atavistics.

Antony Nicholls

Game of Eyes

Pretty women you're floating on high
Playing the game with every guy

A flick of the head, a glance and a look
In the beat of a heart they've swallowed the hook

And then how you tease them as they follow your line
If men had more sense they'd make it a crime

But most men have this weakness and it's deep in their soul
And they're queuing like chimps to score an own goal

Your glances are empty, but men flatter them full
When over their eyes they pull their own wool

Seen from a distance you could laugh 'til you cry
But when it happens to you, you just want to die

Now I've been in the jungle and I've learnt some chimp roles
And I'm telling you now I've scored some great goals!

Allistair Wilson

Your One Night Stand

Now:
we are as before: apart.

After two litres of wine you reached out,
touched me.
First, with words, memories;
and then surprising me
with your hands and body.
Although you do not kiss,
you are gentle, considerate.
you have a fine body,
glowing, warm flesh.

Morning comes.

You appropriate it's grey self-possession.
You do not talk, do not touch, do not look at me.
Last night does not exist.
You have retreated once more,
and so do I.
You are your own man.
I cannot say 'Thankyou'
or 'I enjoyed last night,'
without being an intruder.

Last night had nothing to do with me.
I was irrelevant.
And yet, we lay together.

I wish to celebrate the gentleness of your hands,
the warmth of your body.
I want to shout: 'Do you not remember?'
but have no the masochism
to see again your blank arrogant eyes.

Alastair S Macmillan

Sky-Blue Bedhead

He held a sky-blue bedhead
As he waited for his train.
A small sky-blue bedhead
Tastefully shaped in cane.

The single sky-blue bedhead
Residing on his bed,
Perhaps it's for the spare room
Or for him, since she fled.

I could tell he lived alone,
By the way he held the rungs.
Not for passionate purchase,
But so he could get it home.

He held a sky-blue bedhead
Like a child who was in pain.
Hopeful sky-blue bedhead,
Will his search be in vain?

Ian Smith

In Mute Surrender

You've always tried to tie me in knots
Ensnare me in a turn of phrase
But I've always pulled your fragile bonds apart

Now
Tripping, toppling, tumbling over words
Lead foot into mouth
Full of course with inane professions, persuasions
All ready to spill out

And though I'm troubled by your questions
You're more than thrown by my replies
And though there's a library's worth of knowledge
In every contact of our eyes
We still act unconfident
And feign our surprise

Actions not words
Yet the distinction is blurred
Now we speak more than we talk
And though it seems absurd
Your platitudes were never heard
And we're left with the meaningless of mere words

Yet in the silence
I find a clearer view
The time for eloquence
And loquacity is through
In mute surrender
I see my future lies with you

Stuart Elden

Saturday Night(Mare)

Flashy soul bars, neon lights,
Inadequate men who stop and start fights.
Vacant young things who smoke and chew gum,
Looking like cattle not sexy but dumb.
The bouncers refuse some more likely lads,
Who are out on the pull once again,
And I drink some old bilge,
That makes me feel ill,
But suffer it like a real man.
I'm looking around, and down on the ground,
Are handbags and stiletto heels.
I follow them up to curves and perms,
And wonder 'can all this be real?'
- Enough is enough, OK I'm not tough,
And quite frankly I'm still on my own.
But if Saturday night
Is always this shite,
I'd rather have chips and go home.

Jon Meehan

Rejection

Not for lack of trying
Have I wooed her
Or pursued her
Through the great unknown
Of whether she might return
My favours.
Or spurn them
As one would reject
A slave overindulgent in his labours.

It is that great imponderable known
As Love
That has made a misery
Of my wretched existence.
Such persistence
Should surely be rewarded
By the tender mercies
Of her kiss, a touch, a nod of approval -
But she delights in the sadism of icy gestures.

William Barklam

Soldierboy

I open my eyes.
Outside there's bloodstained streets. This morning
Is like all the rest, bloated like a smelling corpse.
He's here again, the officer in mother's dreams.
Ah . . . these night-time wanderings.

Last night he covered me with silks.
And perfumes to arouse his passions, perhaps!
Or dull the stench of the horrible deeds of day.
Through the remnants of dreams and memories
He calls to me. I'm here again.

Who'd guess this was his war?

I rest a half-open eye on one
Of the many glittering buttons on his handsome jacket.
Bright and gold like six suns
They shine out at me . . . impertinently.

Six suns, and . . . I . . . the only moon.

His lavish hotel . . . I spy him at the sink,
Follow the broken line round the outside of his body.
Large but fine, unusual things happen to the limbs
Beyond a certain size. The bones are huge.

He brought the silk for him, to enhance his own virility,
Set against some notion of delicacy, or frailty.
He brought it so we should be different.
He needn't have bothered.

'I want to cover you with beautiful things,' he said . . .
To make me beautiful where he was, just as he was.
It's an awful truth. I want to stop watching him now
but I can't: His vanity being compulsive.

This man has never killed,
But he knows how to select those that would.

Ann Twenty Seven

In the Pub

Knowing
how to chat up birds
he talks
incessantly

Knowing
men she listens
patiently
an age
old game

Knowing
what's what
underneath
each try
not to notice

Paul Joseph Thompson

No Automated Affair

The days bear,
and unaccounted souls don't know
ah, with you though it's no automated affair.
Hopeful eyes glare and
you are unprepared (or so they say),
but not I
so follow me,
follow me and see
adulthood is not all it's
cracked up to be.
And although you say *No*
I know you dream *Yes* (so say it.)
Your logic leers,
at your cumbersome peers.
A stifled smile (yes I can see it)
that could stretch half a mile (given half a chance)
lays waste to me
but,
'You never gave me all the things
you said you would, to replace all the things
from me that you took.'
But I am here and
here I'll stay waiting to hear your last
dying breath given away (to me).
Yes, I have a heart, but
no soul and though I do dream
it's only for you. The road
of your life begins and
ends with
me.

Sean Isaac Ramnarine

Cornish Memoirs

Shirley Bassey sings
Outside mustard and hemlock mingle
It rains
We play scrabble

I lose
the gull screeches
As I enter its territory
David chants for the dead

It is part of his belief
Thrift grows in abundance
Waves crash against themselves
And we walk on the cliffs

Into the night
Discarding clothes
Releasing our bodies
Cornish air touching

Where others cannot reach
Aroma of sex
Ejaculation completed
Bats fly overhead

Stars shine above
Planets to be seen
Hemlock and mustard grow
And Shirley sings

Martin James Patrick D'Evelin

Sunday Offensive

The television flickers its fits
Cornered like an outpatient relative,
In this era of lasered drabness, with
the everlasting drone of cars outside
Where the neighbours prefer not to know us.

My parents showed me what
to do on these days -
How to pick a fight with the
one you love, arguing for hours
Over God knows what, erecting
impenetrable barriers, entrenched
with silences.

It's a dowry -
an inheritance of bickering
and pointless pain, exploding shells
to kill time and tedium

Until, exhausted, you build up a
laughable climax, catching each other's eyes
and erupting, repairing yourselves
with sex, seducing each other from
drudgery, the genetics of arguing
again and again.

Eleanor Dare

The Woman in my Room

You want some bread then
I said taking my knife
looking at her
seated on the mat
in my room
No! No! No! said she
her high voice
a sigh of the coconut trees outside

sure it was milk she wanted
she looked thirsty and sweaty
pushing away the glass from my hands
her tones the same
No! No! No! like
coming tropical rains

She should be broke then
she looked so sad
and again, again and again
she emphasised: *No! No! No!*
her whole body making rhythms
of delicious meals

and a while later
the tease was gone
neither hunger nor thirst
neither financial want nor sadness
she wanted me
I wanted her

Freddy Macha

Thunder and Lightning

Huddled beneath the houses
Rain deluges upon the street.
Blue lights in a distant sky
Have become a storm raging
Directly above the passing canals.

Out of the darkness in sudden flashes
A face coolly calm
Looks out at the discharging fury
Released in sudden bolts of fire.
There may be safety and comfort
In the haven of the music night
But the downpouring rain allows
No movement. It forces the ears
To hear its beat upon the empty streets.
See the water of the canal churned
Into a target for the hurtling drops
Of heavy loaded clouds torn
By the electric storm. Thunder
Echoes the street, dazed by rain.

It is safe here, quiet, a shelter
In the open but a haven. Peace,
You may search for that everywhere,
Yet possess it all the time. Stop.
Listen to the rain, it is all clear,
Soon you will have to leave
Purged of all the trials you have borne.

The old jazz fans with darting eyes
Announce they have found
No comfort in age, they have not
Seized the hour.
The music of the dance
Sweeps another hall, a church of the moment
Where surprise is the partner of desire.

David Ryan

Apple Bobbing

My teeth grip
smooth skin
slide away

head over heels
I'm breathless

sweet taste
on my tongue
goads me on

I drink

mouthfuls
of water
I don't want
or need

coming up
gasping

I try again
and try again
and try
again

green apples
bob around
my submerged
head

tantalising

out

of

reach

Emma Greengrass

The Silence

The day's routine,
Remains unchanged.
The gentle touch,
Throughout the day.
That says 'We are',
Where once was 'I am',

And the special touch,
That lingers, strokes.
The look she gives,
No need for words.
That signals time,
For love.

Grant Alan Wickman

Seduction

I kneel to get the file
and my head is at the height
of your mini-skirted thighs.

I rest my hand on the floor,
the little finger touching
the high heel of a red shoe.

Divided by inches
a hardened cock
could bridge the gap
between us
across which angels walk.

Unseen I lick my lips
and you fidget.
Your seamed tights brush together
as you walk away,
the sound of wings
beating in my head.

You'll be back.

Already,
below your mind,
beneath your heart,
I hear the squelch of succulence.

Anthony Knight

Your Ghost

Your ghost is in my garden

My new gardener
does not realise this
and is disturbed
Disturbed
by sudden deaths
of seeming fertile foliage

Your ghost is in my streams
shall I block the water
flatten vegetation
Desert myself

My new gardener seduces me
with designs on my landscape
and I listen
Dreaming of new shrubbery
Ghost free.

Jessie Gordon

Untitled

Easing up the back of your rough tartan skirt,
Split down one side and held with a
large metal pin,
I slip my fingers under the elastic of your
thick woollen tights
And grab cool pink flesh as my hands
work downwards.
Pressing you to me, the heat on my leg
is always a sharp surprise.
I have the whole Universe in my grasp.
I'm a god.
All power and all knowledge is mine.

Chris Ridgway

Tour of Beauty

At the double
Up in arms!
Hup, two, three,
Battle alarm!
Enemy encroaching,
(Girl approaching),
Fall out, fall out,
Mr High Flyer!

Advance with caution,
At the ready
(It's your duty
This tour of beauty)
Finger steady,
Aim, and . . .

'Hi ya.'

Terry Egan

High Society Call-Girl

My client is watching me undress
Paying me five hundred pounds and nothing less
Slowly stripping off my school uniform
My man from the Manor Born
Exposing my smooth body all over
My client's acting like a Casanova
I'm a girl, healthy and clean
Living out his child-woman dream
My client gives me mega money
I'm his living Sadie-doll Honey
I'll never ever tell the newspapers
About this tycoon's kinky, fetish capers

Jelly Bean Gold

Two Species

Two species
Two races
Two forms of
loveliness and light.
My eyes are bloodshot
and thirsty. Can I see your loveliness
tonight?

James W Harper

Adult Games

It started as brothers and sisters
in a cottage on the borders;
they cooked themselves a grown-up dinner

sat by the log fire cuddling
(it's an easy game
when you don't much fancy one another).

Mothers and fathers have prams and kids;
and, far away in sunny woods, no harm
could come of pretending that too.

Back in town it was doctors and nurses;
she had the baby chucked away -
it couldn't cope with urban life.

Tim Dowley

The Morning After the (One) Night (Stand) Before

You know the ritual
It begins with a long hot bath
Stay under the shower
For an hour
And scrub your skin 'til it hurts
Add powder, add perfume
Wear freshly laundered clothes
It is in vain
His smell will still remain
It was not on your skin
It is within
Like the bitter memory
Of urgent sordid fumbling in the dark
That cannot be justified
However hard you try
You thought you needed company
You thought you needed warmth
You thought the price was flesh
Not self-respect
You realise now
You try to blame the wine
The mood, the music and the night
But nothing helps
And nothing alters facts
Before he left
You guessed that you'd been cheated
Alone
You see quite clearly
You were fucked

Ruby Alexander

One Enchanted Evening

Our eyes meet across a crowded room.
I think 'This is a man of my dreams.'
Tall, dark, slim with an educated air.
Confidence *sans* arrogance, it seems.

I watch him as he talks attentively with his friends,
Not afraid to share of himself.

Our eyes meet and then again.
He stands up, my view's complete.
With a relaxed and easy walk he strolls my way.
He's here. At my feet. There's no retreat.

Close up this guy's too good to be true
Even his accent's French.

My knees turn to jelly.
My confidence melts in the beating of my heart
'Stay on the fringes' I tell myself.
'Whatever you do please don't engage.'
Thank God! Here's my bus!
It's safer this way.

Whatever my intentions
I don't take easily to passion.

Tontschy Gerig

The Experience of Love

Your soft gentle touch upon my skin
Reaching, soul deep, touches me within.
Your arms, your breasts, your soft sweet mound
Wrap no body, yet bind my soul around.
Your arms that cradle, cradle nought,
But my mind's tender thought.

Each push, each thrust, each stroke,
Obeys words you never spoke.
For long, my love, have I understood
How you use my manhood.
How you so willingly yield to me
Yet yield to yourself, for I *am* thee.

So love's great soul goes round and round
Forever lost, forever found.

John Baker

A Happy Man

In love I am
A happy man,
I taught
the thought
that brought
your heart,
I fought
so taut
the line that caught
your soul,
I sought
I wrought
our love,
In short,
In love I am,
A happy man.

Nicholas Redfearn

Satyr

You knew that when you called I would be there
And I travelled through the night,
Pushing wildly through the evening rain,
Taking chances on the lonely roads
In my eagerness and longing to
Meet my Prince of Darkness.

I looked into your eyes and knew that I was lost;
My mind no longer was my own
As your caressing fingers sought to steal
My every thought and longing that was locked inside
my heart.

The feelings that I craved I knew that you could
give;
That you could take me to the heights
With your games of pain and pleasure
Played upon my willing body
That belonged to you that night.

That night I hoped, would be the first
Of many that we would share;
I could not resist my storming heart
Nor thoughts of caution to beware.

Mercedes

Thoughts

My life begins, I eat, procreate, go into old,
age, die, my life is over, to metamorphose,
into something else, the human thought,
process, never quite knowing the truth,
for living, the philosopher persuades his,
student to climb the cathedral spire,
to view, by his own senses, the smallness,
of the landscape, of the Cosmos, maybe the,
inconsequentiality of the Cosmos, Wittgenstein,
decides, makes up his mind, that probably
there are no superhuman beings, we're
answerable to, but upon my death, what
happens to my thought process, does it face,
oblivion, here in the present, I think,
why can we be so cruel, are we nothing,
but evolution of one species to the next,
does it matter if we're good or bad,
like a tiger do we contain both,
have a cunning to survive, God and Devil,
are they but words, dreamt up by mortals,
Bacon's pictures' creatures howl out,
what is the meaning of their wretched,
existence, Rembrandt self portraits reveal,
what he may have looked like, the personality
although one that was brutal and kind,
Hancock's idiot rebel artist, gets on with,
the present, to create a hideous, sculpture.

Rob Williams

Liaisons

She encaged
I tightened
She pushed
I pumped
She laughed
I sighed
She scratched
I squeezed
And as climax came,
We both cried out for more.

The doors of celibacy being pushed aside!

Marcus McKee

Wasted Gifts, Love's Overflow

Worked-up
by such pent-up desire
he seeks to quench
the raging fire
which blazes deep within.

Each day
he gives a gift to her
a piece of him,
from him, for her,
each seed a gift for her.

Yet she
knows none of what goes on,
this one-way love,
this love of one
who feels himself for her.

Each gift,
with care wrapped in paper,
he wants so much
to give to her,
instead is flushed away.

These wasted gifts,
Love's overflow,
are hidden away,
so who's to know
the pipes are full of them . . .

John Scopes

Initial Glimpse

ink has spilled upon your shirt
vivid blue splash against the light
fabric cleaving the skin that stretches
to pull me through descending night

clustered strands refract and fall
across that sketch who shapes your face
where stories await beneath the lines
with my thumb imprint I would trace

icy cubes collide your knuckles clench
tumbling liquid will reflect my eyes
search through mirrored fog to rest
upon your soul where desire lies

your eyes of misty dusk colours and white
fluffy clouds where I shall float on air
sunlight will reach out fingertips
warmth enough to stroke my hair

feel the fluttering abdomen that shades
tumbling questions scalding inside
shall I thread my way amidst the thong
to you or here within my throat hide

Helen J Macnaughtan

Untitled

every word.
we sat on the grass.
tiny spiders ran across our hands.
a translucent web
a thread invisible
binding you recumbent
your blue shirt.
numb sunshine.
I remember every word.

Hilaire

Untitled

I fell in lust with you the first time I clocked yer
just down from Margarets
Cambridge
a card carrying deconstructionist
not for me though too pretty too bright
I resolved to be cold brusque
it covered the pang and made you pay somehow
good game good game
still people must talk and we did
oh God
there must be a God
that face is no mere biological accident
that face blazes soft child joy laugh wit juices
I want it I want you
now
it is a funny thing
what I want I convince myself I do not want
when I get it I find I do not want it
it just became a lump of raw liver

Martin Wheeler

Again

You said it was love
I got bored - again

You tried to get too close
I got scared - again

You took my space
I panicked - again

You were broke
I paid - again

You adored me
I stopped trying - again

I finished it
You got upset and cried - again

I was alone
Free and happy - again

You were really sweet today
I want you back - again

I should've known
This would happen - again

Martin A Swain

Bourgeois Sex

First though invoked
with eyes undress
her hair and thigh
then breast caressed
her smile aloof
she gets on top
no time has passed
but all has stopped . . .

Herb Richard

Unspoken

you lookin good you still have that beard
you still have that grey you two years older
but you lookin good
you still have those too-blue eyes
you still have that bear-hug
and those shades
seems like
your flirtatious tongue gone some
but hell maybe I aint . . . lookin good
or two years harder on me than you?
well hey we never did quite
get it together
and you more married this time
than ever
but
man
you lookin good
you still got that grin
that you-aint-foolin-me-you-want-it-
grin   yep
sure do

Jill Dawson

Nature's Lovers

Your whispered words, spoken in earnest
Became my souvenirs - the promise of a kiss
My previous resistance, now so paper-thin
Completely buried within a thick, sensual mist

As I stand before you, heart clenched in a fist
Feeling naked, exposed - my lips as yet unkissed
The wrapping of my body slowly peel away
And in your arms, like the trees above, I sway

Mindless want as was this, I had yet to feel
At the altar of your love I felt my desire kneel
Fiery light bursting upon the darkening hour -
My body's surrender to your unharnessed power

Sated, I lay upon the sheet of leaf and moss
As the clock ticked away and the minutes flew
I felt as though I'd suffered a momentous loss
When the warmth of your body from mine withdrew

Fresh from the onslaught of your urgent caress
My surface from the stormy sea of passion was slow
Your racing pulse still throbbed upon my chest
Your life essence escaped me from a portal below

Short-lived was that moment when our hearts were entwined
In a coupling that was the cause of the Robin's blush
The languages of body and mind defined
Awash with the love dew in the grasses so lush

Juliet Cooper

Swallow Love

I feel the sweet lick of your tired teeth
Ripping my heart on the edge of Lovers' Leap

Chew me
Chew me
I'm a masochistic Jew, me

Roll me in your mouth
Roll me in your head
Roll me with your tongue
My nerves are fockin' shreds

C'mon bite my outstretched hand
Masticate my breast
Eat my brain with your smile
Hey, be my fockin' guest

No joke:
Just place your mouth on mine
Just place your mouth on mine
C'mon just place your mouth on mine
No joke:
Your mouth
On
Mine

Desire needn't be hollow

If Love is there, it will follow

You've chewed me well

For fock's sake

Swallow...
Kerry Shale

Among my Corots

I point three Japanese toward the Titians,
Resume my post.
Watch for Magda.

She touches my earring like an amulet,
A martyr's wound, a lover's charm.
In the Sculpture Room we duck behind
A Henry Moore. Here,
Among the Corots,
There is no niche for our smeary idylls.

I check the Thermo-hygrograph;
A fever-chart of sticky breath,
Measure of their ecstasy.

The man before the Corot comes
Every afternoon; in silk cravat and polished shoes.
Always the same picture:
Feathery trees against a sky
Of rancid blue. He weeps
Sometimes.

I cross to the Seurat, stand up close,
Play join-the-dots . . .

Murmur of innumerable BAs . . .

We tread the streets in a three-legged race,
Embrace.
I take her on the Embankment, a hurried stand-up job.
She clutches at my hair, my neck,
Tells me the earring suits me.

The spindly tree beside me, half uprooted,
Wavers in the wind, its leaves
Feathery against the sky.

I taste the salt.

David Rose

Kissing Through a Pain of Glass

For sixty moon benighted months he fanned the flames of hope
And sent her muffled mystic runes in cheap brown envelopes
Believing it was possible with playful taunts and smiles
To bridge the gap of five years and eleven thousand miles

Five years of waiting, watching changes, constructing strange designs
An expertise was nurtured writing in between the lines
He chose each thought, each syllable with devious delight
So skilled he soon believed he could convince her black was white

He conjured worlds of fantasy, he promised her the earth
He guaranteed her everlasting love (for what it's worth)
He waited for her swift replies and hung on every word
And searched in vain for 'I love you' (the words he'd never heard)

Examining each line of prose a dozen times or more
But all he found were warm regards which cut him to the core
Distraught, he never lost his faith, though deep within there burned
A passion that he knew for sure could never be returned

A trip was planned, his heartbeat raced, the chance he'd waited for
With careful words used face-to-face she'd fall for him once more
Unless his plans were stifled by that great unspoken fear
(That poetry is meaningless to those that cannot hear)

Abandoning all notions of failure or rebuff
He carved with simple curves and strikes an endless song of love
So sad, his masterpiece would only win him second place
For handsome words cannot compete with an unknown suitor's face

For when the rendezvous occurred he realised at last
One cannot write one's future nor recompose the past
Their fate was locked beyond his grasp, written in the stars
Resigned to that of lovers kissing through a pane of glass

Peter Michael Rosenberg

Meanwhile, Upstairs at the Party

    He   She
    Hi!   Shy
    Hold   Shouldn't
    Heat (of the moment)   Surely (not happening!)
but He'd   so Shattered
    Heel   Shame
    Hide   Shaking
    Shorry! (drunk)   Hell (go to!)

Fizz Fieldgrass

Unmarried Birth

Unable to love, unable to care
Grab his ride, pay his fare
He costs so much in heart and soul
Your naked lust, his only goal

You'll want him more, the worse he acts
He'll always lie, avoid the facts
In your bed, he takes your heart
He leaves so soon, you fall apart

He's never there, you never learn
When he's away you always yearn
Many girls far and wide
Your name is lost on morning tide

Sends you flowers, nameless card
Soon you're dropped fast and hard
Broken heart, now you're plastered
Now you know that man's a *Bastard!*

Nik Hussey

Old Hand - New Boy

Me, old hand, making the tea, turned and saw, you, the new boy,
my Mills & Boon hero made flesh.
With shock, I dropped the tea.
You, new boy, turned on me and smiled.
I felt foolish, embarrassed, confused but in love.
I went home that night oblivious to the rain, the litter and the
crowded bus.
Uncertain, I looked for advice in
'How to get your man!'
'Are you sexy enough?' and
'Ten steps to better orgasms',
devouring these articles as a new convert would her bible.
I told my sister, my mom and then phoned all my friends.
You were a God they all agreed.
Next morning, a bathroom prisoner.
New hair, new eyes, new toes, new me.
No old hand but new girl!
I raced to work, eager to see you.
I heard you shout hello.
I turned and smiled and there you were
hand in hand with *your* Mills & Boon man.
I turned and wept.
My 'Barbara Cartlands,' were never like this.

Eden Louise Mulliner

Caller

The line goes dead, sudden silence,
The sounds of that voice was laughter; violence,
Should I have said those words? But this is
just playing,
Games with our heads and words that we're
saying.

The next day you think at a time you are
free,
Whether that caller is thinking of me,
Telling yourself that person is thinking,
The same in your mind, but we still go on
living.
Hoping for ringing which never arrives.
Forgetting that person is ever alive.

Tracey Beth

Man Menu

(for Karen Fleming)

As we sip at our drinks: my lager, your whisky,
You toy with the menu laying on our table.
Whilst wondering whether to eat here - or later?
I suggest an alternative to make you frisky.

(For starter - to please your erogenous palette)

A duo of well-strapped, well-hung young males
To which ingredients you add sex and spice,
Tossing my way every favourite position,
Causing that sparkle to glint in your eyes.

Whilst my mind conjures more passion-filled dishes,
You thrust (with added sauce) towards the juicy male courses,
No Provence snails, but Chippendales - served
By the baker's dozen - to enrapture your senses.

(Though I suggest that they be served without baby oil
Which kills all sex scent and spoils the sweet thrill)

Intensely preparing our erotic menu,
Two differing scenes form in two lustful minds,
Desires of yourself being satisfied by service,
Myself playing voyeur to this pornographic stew.

Suddenly, as you offer me another Rothmans,
I question whether this is for post-coital reasons,
Together: we laugh, we kiss and we smile
Both throwing aside all our inhibitions.

(Whilst wondering how long will be the wait
Before I'm the main course delivered on your plate?)

Sacha Colgate

Croydon Sandstorm

Here we lie beside each other;
Lifting up the smooth outskirts of love,
You and me swearing this is truth -
We both lie in bed.

As we lie
Our bodies become grainy,
Shifting into multitudinous pieces
Sharp with senses.

Held in isolating light so long,
We no longer generate shadows;
We are sand, we are hot, flesh
We bake, we squeeze moisture dry

And you, sand beside me
Storm on me
Cover me, sand on sand mating,
In a desert the size of a bed.

Soon you shimmer away in a mirage.
I sift out sideways
Into the narrow, querulous sunlight
Of a drowned summer.

Soft rain makes sand scream,
Covering it in taut skin.
Casting dark, senseless shadows,
Winter will come early this year.

David R Morgan

Untitled

12.27, Regent Street.
I was waiting for you
      while watching all the girls go by.
Arousing my interest
      a minidressed beauty
           came out of the blue.
I looked on in wonder
      and then I looked again
           and noticed she was
                you.

Ian Mole

Calling

calling up
old girlfriends
at midnight
on Saturday nights
is fun
if it rings with
no answer
you know
they're still on
their own
they haven't found
Mr Right yet
so maybe
they'll give
Mr Wrong
another
try.

Steve Verrall

Divinations

I write your name across the page in thick
black script. My own fits snugly underneath
- a trick I learnt at school - to slash in pairs

twinned letters, two sibling Ss,
the double Es and with the sum that's left
count he loves me, loves me not . . .

My world is made of signs. Magpies for sorrow
and for joy. I avoid the pavement cracks,
disregard the news of world events

for Patrick Walker's Star Signs. Add dates
and times in significant contortions. If I could
I'd read the tea leaves in my mug, lay out old

chickens' bones, hang up dry seaweed to gage
the drift and shift of things. Like an obi-man
peeling back loose flaps of skin to see

the flesh beneath, I peer into dim tomorrows
to check if you're hidden there. I'm bored
with waiting for something to happen

trying to conjure you from this bald white
page. Don't offer me enigmas, Chinese puzzles
and conundrums simply to avoid

the pain of real communion. At night
in secret, I slip silver coins
through my fingers - a ten piece drachma

kept for luck - and in the yin and yang
of hexagrams try to decipher the future's
script to see if you could love me.

Sue Hubbard

Three O'Clock in the Morning

Tired.
Head throbbing.
Music pumping.
Want to go home.
Ladies toilets.
Face a mess.
Hair a mess.
Life a mess.
On my own.
Want to go home.
Disco's whirling.
Bar swirling.
Skirts' twirling.
Too much wine.
Don't feel fine.
Apathy's mine.
Always the same.
When I play this game.
Out for the night.
Start off alright.
A good time in sight.
Surrounded by friends.
Or so It seems.
Drink too much.
Say too much.
They desert me.
Doesn't hurt me.
Or so It seems.
I've got those three o'clock in the morning blues.

Lisa Bush

Dance Around me

Dance around me and laugh your cackle
How wrong I've been in the things I've said
Ask no questions and see no love there
Vent your anger and cut me dead

Dance around me and laugh your cackle
Strangle the spider to free the fly
What used to be care is now codependence
What used to be love is an excuse to pry

Dance around me and laugh your cackle
For if I cry you can always say
The salt of my tears isn't your problem
Haemorrhage quietly and out of my way

Dance around me and laugh your cackle
We sat in a church and we whispered a vow
You bought me a diamond and I believed you
But that was then and now is now

Beverly J Kemp

One Night Stand

I don't take no for a question,
Although the answer is normally yes.
If you give me your daytime number,
I promise I'll give you less.
My heart's as big as Frisco,
It loves that Free Love dance,
So pull me up at the disco
And let's have a quick romance.
You're an evening primrose amongst my nettles,
You're the silver, gold and bronze of metals,
You're the Beatles' girl who drove their car,
You're Patrick Moore's favourite star,
You're in the mirror in the morning,
You're in every dream I dream,
When you're here you stop me yawning
You're my chocolate chip ice cream.
So wear me, snare me, downright Huggy Bear me,
I'll be your court jester, your Uncle Fester,
Your gay, white, animal right, save the whale protester,
Unzip me, strip me, hold me tight and grip me,
Take me out late at night and Elmlea double whip me,
Stop, and buy me, try me, oil up a pan and fry me,
Put me in Italics and ball-point underline me,
Get down to the river and sinker, hook and line me,
Pull me from the water
and slip me in your net,
And I promise this one night stand
Will be the one we should forget.

Jason Raper

Cruise Bar

Propping up the bar - their egos all aglow
Won't you take me home tonight -
    whatever you said your name was.
You try and listen above the noise,
    but a philosophical conversation is not much of an ice
                                                            breaker.
And the flashing lights prevent you from looking too closely
    at your prospective bed partner.
Your place or mine?
Let's dance the night away first.
How can I ditch this creep?
What if no-one else wants you?
Can't bear to go home alone.
So you drink a bit more, perhaps he's not that bad looking,
    perhaps I won't feel so cheap.
His hands on me, accidentally?
Shall I buy you another drink or shall we go home now?
Am I incapable yet?
Hold on, I remember him from last week,
    he looked older then, who was the boy he was with?
A nameless face like me.
He's not looking at me too closely, I wonder why?
How can I refuse? Sound so naive?
    Just one more drink?
Yeah, then we'll go home.
Don't switch the lights off here,
    don't switch them on at home.
There's another nameless boy in the corner,
    maybe he'll be taken home next week.
Maybe, I'll take him home next week!

Sue Bowley

My Bath Ran Away With a Gurgle

When I'm alone,
And I've nothing to do,
I sit in my bath,
It reminds me of you,
You think I'm in jest,
Well, I tell you it's true,
My bath runs away . . . with a gurgle.
As I look at you now,
You look nonplussed,
To me it was love,
To you it was lust,
Please can I ask,
What happened to trust?
My bath ran away . . . with a gurgle.
So, go off with that monster,
That you call Wayne,
Off to Stoke Poges,
Don't come back again,
Don't utter a word,
You don't need to explain,
Just run away . . . with that gargoyle.
I don't want to depress you,
Or make you feel down,
But I'll tell you something,
Before you leave town,
I'm filling my bath tub,
And I'm going to drown,
I'm going away . . . with a gurgle.

T J Carpenter

Dancing Days

On polished floor
the labours of love,
portrayed in oils
and bonded promises;
the music swells
as you rise above
the cut glass walls
and cocktail sculpture,
holding each golden
word to light your way.
Whispered caresses
of sweet distraction,
little clouds of madness
waft around the senses,
to fritter all reason away.
As time winds down
and the doors are thrown back;
two by two you make
the night your own.

John Steer

Coming of Age

She was too young, I was too old.
She wanted to buy, I was already sold.
More potbelly,
Than pot of gold.

An odd couple in apparent harmony,
She brought out the father in me.
Kept me warm with
Kisses by the sea.

What she saw in me remains a mystery,
Perhaps she collected antiques,
Or studied living history.
Maybe she gave her love
Out of sympathy.

I believed all that she told me then;
About preferring more mature
And distinguished looking men.
No wonder she became
Such a good comedienne.

It was over as quick as it had began.
She had her fun with me,
Then found a younger man.
They found their love
In the back of a baker's van.

In the book of my life,
She fills one painful page.
She left my love,
On a dark and empty stage.
Just a young girl;
Who'd barely come of age.

David Read

At Browns Just for Fun

Through loud music and smoke
In dense odour of sweat and Best Bitter
Over half moons of male skulls
I saw a woman - dance and undress.

All too soon
She had nothing, but
High heels and some pride inside.

From behind
Those greasy mirrors spat back
Merciless images of us - the low crowd.

Through her spread thighs
I looked
Over dull faces into my red eyes.

Until a pint
clinking clanking with petty money
threw me back
Into a world of supply and demand.

Ernst Schlögelhofer

RSVP 2020 AD

Don't you find it terribly exciting,
butting through space in present company?
'I do'. Lifting his mauve lace veil, the bride,
- extravagant even at this moment -

saw destiny mirrored in his green eyes.
Crossing all the boundaries of gender,
passport no proof of your identity,
time was passed and the future unsettled

by an instant kiss of eternity.
You a twenty-first century being?
Parallel-dimension homespun hero?
Chromosomes shone to quantum-leap your mind

and activate the hidden switch. Memory.
You wear high heels, your face a made-up
mask of polymorphous haute couture; you step
down the corridors of time striking sparks!

This is the confetti hour. Sprinkle. Click!
Photographs trick into the emulsion
of memory their colour shutter proof.
Like follows like towards infinity.

Hazel Lezah

Untitled

Kiss me
Lick me
Lift me

Suck me
Fuck me
Rough me

Wet me
Get me
Let me

Make me feel
Make me real
Make me steal

Make me come
Make me dumb
Make me some

Let me stay
Let me pay
Let me lay

Smother me
Cover me
Lover me

Really
Nearly

Ryeli Thomas

The Guide to Love Technique

I was never fond of girls
White socks, braces, freckles and curls
Just the thought made me shudder
Of a kiss with the suction of a cow's udders!

Then with the force of a falling slab of stone
I was hit by a head-on collision with testosterone
And filled with a fresh sense of desire
I went in search with 'affection to hire'.

In glossy-ad clothes stood scrawny me
I set out like a radio dial looking for a lost frequency
Breathing in, confident, in search of cool
I counted my steps on the street - I wouldn't look a fool.

Then in the corner of my eye
Long legs, flowing curls, a gleaming smile
Was the female equivalent of the FA Cup
Were my hands the ones to lift her up?

I ambled up to her, she said softly 'Yes?'
I hoped whatever I said - she'd guess
So I said 'Do you come here often?'
And only the passage of time has helped it forgotten.

I hadn't been a bounder or a cad
But I'd definitely let slip the chance I'd had
Now I don't speak to women - I can only squeak
Where was 'The Guide To Love Techniques'?

Gary Marks

Bath Time

You are sitting in the bath
Between my legs
And I touch the skin of your back
Through the flannel clinging there
Yes warm to the finger ends
The dampness of the pockmarked flannel
Against the firmness of your butter skin
I lean over to lick now.

The rivulets of milky water
Free themselves from the flannel
And find their way into the crevices of your spine
To meet the gasps of steam rising.

This lazy suspension of our enfolded bodies
In the lateness of a Sunday morning
Is a sauna for our very souls.

Water holds us to the truth
In this tub.

Our throats must work hard now
As our sated purring turns into eager talking.
Open, tender, angry, free
Our criss cross words caress
In muted echo above our heads-
A music of speech on iron and water.

Without our bodies against each other
Back to chest
My hands wet under the curves of your breasts
In counterpoint near motionless
We would not be able to talk like this.

Round the corner the church bells ring in the afternoon
And we think of things for lunch.
You stand up to soap your body down
As cooling water laps against my ribs.
Time to get out soon.

Paul Richards

Mr Heppenstall - Optician

Waiting in the blackness for Randolph Scott to show, I fumble with
a dainty crocheted hankie, knot my guts. Expectant? you bet!
'Just keep looking straight ahead, focus on the red and green.'
Ah yes, the opticians not the picture-house; I peer.

A click and hum, projection light-beam on,
and Mr Heppenstall at my ear, a glove puppet of a man.
An inch, no more, above my skin, snorting,
chest heaving, our brows touch at last.

For ninety minutes (feature length) our passion melts the screen,
all-conquering love, against the odds, my leading man and I,
until at last with climax near he checks and states 'That's
fine Mrs Clarke, no problem there.' The house lights come up.

I vacate the auditorium, dust the deceit from my coat,
and slip out into the sodden brickwork of Wombwell, South Yorks.
We ride the forty-seven with worn-out shoppers, my guilt and I, for
it's home to Ralph, the evening news, the dog and egg and chips.

Nick Woodall

Mr B. Astard
(A Love Poem Of Sorts)

      A false I.D. and a claim of love for me
You fed me all along, sweet meats of deceit
Why did you think . . . suppose I was so strong?
      To allow my heart to break was, clearly, *my* mistake
I trusted you, your depth of sincerity
Thus committing my sentiments to parchment, for posterity
      Subsequently, upon the shock and gradual detection
Of your ignominious valour
The selfless complexion, of my unilateral affection
'Instantly' altered pallor.
      Having purported, to love me
You philandered (though I still pandered)
And cavorted, 'blamelessly'
Or so you said. In my dreams
Harsh, of a sudden, you towered
As the ultimate, the consummate, coward.
      Your words and motions, perennially sleek
Your manner, on cue, conveniently meek
Not before time, my honeyed perceptions, soured
My wombly trusting nature, abrasively scoured.
      He who I perceived
To be unique, the one who cleaved
To me, as his partner
Actually, consciously, cannily, deceived.
      Possessing every seemly credential
An abundance of amorous potential
Yet you blew it -
Now I've gone through it . . . and survived.
      To personally devise
And self-craft,
Your own demise
Occasioned by sundry ignoble lies
While *twigging* for your ego, a raft
Proves one thing, for sure, is true -

I was *far too good* for you.
You'll never select one so apt, in *my* lieu
I wish you ever witch in Christendom
You deserve them all, you profligate bum.
      Life's too short
To consider love, a sport
Go drown you puerile insecurities
And purge your character of its impurities.
      I'll live my life with comprehensive ease
Now you're finito. Dealt with - Completo
Me - Maud Gonne; You - Yeats
Me - Doing the ditching; You - Gates!

Denise O'Kelly

Doggerel Fashion

Twisted lust was all it took
That, and a few sly letters
Twenty years and soaked in sin
I really should have known better

God and whiskey protect the fool
From your stockings' rustling sigh
And that shiny, silver suspender clip
Enthroned on your queenly thigh!

Animated classics
Inside a shot silk blouse
Teasey, Pleasey, Cheesey
The man becomes a mouse

Bewitched, bewildered, befuddled
Another Good Man Gone
Give him the slip, wear your skirt on your hip
And meet me later on

Eyes like nuclear fusion
Burning spears of blue
Legs like American highways
Bring me back to you

A smile to break the heart of a saint
Melting butter on a crumpet
Park your morals by the door
Love me now, sweet strumpet!

Dress it up in Sunday clothes
Send it out to church
I'll worship at your holy shrine
Lust left me in the lurch!

George M Frew

Shoulder Ride

Young girl
reveal yourself to me
doe eyed love
of furtive glance
so nervous
I eye your calves
their perfect symmetry
of muscular existence
even higher
my eyes will travel
to firm white thighs
around my neck
restrain themselves
In ways you never knew
I lower you carefully
to the ground
and there you stand
standing easy
legs slightly akimbo
young innocence
not yet knowing
of your sensuality.

Myk Johnson

Untitled

I stand and wait
and watch
cut open
on the narrow slopes of bone
that are your face.
Bleeding and blissful
on the stained South London pavement
I have come to buy
potatoes, carrots, leeks
Cheap. Filling. Sensible.
Your hands, pale as mushrooms
twist at the brown paper bags.
I surface through layers
of impossibility
to find that I want to lick
your eyebrows, reach breathless
palms out to the deer
in your eyes
and lead it far away from artificial grass.
But I am the captured one now
trapped at the head of the queue
I look at you.
You smile
and out of my mouth
spill strawberries and peaches
apricots, cherries, melons and nectarines.
Wandering home with an empty purse
to an empty flat
arms full of ripe red juice
I hear myself think:
Yes. This is my vow -
I shall eat only fruit salad
live forever
and finally leave my husband.

Kim Farley

Free

That afternoon, you laughed so much
telling us about your holiday beau -
a widower with the blarney touch.

You said it was just a mild fling
with lots of laughs and ravenous chat,
a little adventure on the wing.

And your seventy-five years shook,
ironing out their creases;
you swore you wouldn't have to look

further for someone perfect to love
and be loved by, your voice almost shy.
But nothing could move

you to remarry - 'that leap for the sky'
you called it, and he, bemused,
couldn't understand why

you chose to live alone
now - after all these years
wanting a life of your own.

Katherine Gallagher

Johnny

You are a bastard I'm afraid it's true
That's my considered point of view
Despite your gauche, endearing charm
Brains and easygoing calm
And your endless sex appeal
You do not think, you do not feel.
I loved too well upon reflection
A man named after contraception.

Rochelle Levy

Love in Bloom

One day whilst sitting in the park,
By a beautiful flower bed;
I thought I saw some movement,
Then spied two tiny heads.

On close examination,
Two handsome ducks I saw;
One a pretty female gal,
The other, a male, she adored.

They sat side by side, just looking ahead,
As quiet as quiet could be;
In flowers that surrounded them,
like a beautiful deep blue sea.

An hour went by, but still they sat.
It was soon time for me to depart.
I often wonder, when love took place,
And if they are still sweethearts.

Ruby Anderson

The Quirks of Human Nature

If I could be content with now and leave the ifs to wiser minds;
If I could learn to love my lot with less dreams passed set centre-stage,
Perhaps I'd focus more on fact and put less stress on theory . . .
(And perhaps I'd sprout a halo and be obscenely cheery).

How often did we girls meet up to muse our fates as lesser beings?
How often did we share neglect and feed our doubts with drink-stoked gloom?
For then, it seemed, to catch a mate - (at least one worthy of that name) -
Was the essence of existence and the antidote to shame.

But should the scent of man approach and a likely tryst confront us;
Should faith bespoke a date á deux with much to rouse the senses
Then see the transformation in the once-despondent stares!
And beware the force of rivalry amongst the ardent mares!

If we could time the smile just right whilst dropping eyes to heighten charm;
If we could hold the blasé pose whilst making sure to block his path,
Perhaps he'd pause a second, perceiving the object of his dreams?
No . . . too soon the gorgeous back had turned, immune to cunning schemes.

And yet, should some pubescent wretch presume to copy female tricks;
Should some excuse for manhood waft *aware* amongst Medusa's throng,
(Whether or not he proffered gifts; mellifluous phrases soft to the ear,)
For certain he'd be banished - by way of a heel applied to his rear.

Thus when at *last* love slapped our cheeks (as often is the case):
When at last *he* came along and did not slink to fairer sides,
Unusually it was neither his face, nor his words, that drew us together . . .
I best recall the infectious laugh and the jacket of putrid leather.

Now I'm starting to value the gifts of life and learning from past mistakes,
I'm better at living the moment and returning the love that I take.
Yet, whilst I study the virtuous route, can anyone meanwhile explain . . .
Why it is I frequently wish myself just a *single girl* again?!

Karen Simpson-Harris

In my Lover's Bed, Arising

You have feathered me lightly
to the mornings rush -
from the velvet caressing night
to the honeyed kiss of dawn.
The barest touch of your fingertips
brushes sand from my eyes
that dried from evenings tears
and falls away as
stardust, feathers, old joy.
The pressing of your heartbeat to mine,
the breath of my mouth upon yours,
to whisper-sing your name
in my secret garden,
whilst rapture on the wing
soars uncaged the sky.

V N Jacobs

Louise Loves Melting Candles

Louise loves melting candles
And watching the wax drip
Onto my frowning forehead, rolling down my nose
And setting on my lip

I pretend to understand
What she's implying when she says -
'A girl needs more than just love
and security these days.'

As I fall asleep
I'm sure I hear her weep

Louise loves melting candles
And letting the red wax roll
Onto my neck and across my chest
Searching for my soul

I try to understand
As the hot wax drips and burns
If it's excitement or enlightenment
Or for power that she yearns

Pray for poor Louise
And then please pray for me

I love listening to Louise
Feeling her warm tears roll
Off her chin, onto my shoulder
Burning up my soul

Hamish Gane

Space Shag

Agog in ether,
Drifting,
Floating,
Dreaming,
Pissed.

The infinite gravitational pull,
Of a black hole.
No escape.

You are my Venus,
Space Shag,
Or are you,
Just a stupid,
Fucking,
Cow.

Zinc Oberon

The Erotic Journey

The van races by, straining and pulling,
desperate to complete its task.
The driver sits behind the wheel,
eyes squinting to see the sacred road.
The van snakes its way into the dense forest,
knowing that the special place shall be reached soon.
The van nuzzles inward, parting the folds of darkness,
the road dampens with light smooth drops of moisture.
The van encounters a small hill,
the road ripples with the first wave of pleasure.
Now the van moves with the motion,
at first slowly, then with increasing momentum.
The van reaches the crux of the hill,
the road shakes and writhes.
The van waits, poised at the crux,
inching forward,
the road eager and effervescent.
Suddenly the van thrusts forth, beginning the rapid descent,
the road cracks like a whip,
pulling and pushing, desperate to engulf the van.
The van reaches top speed,
the road and van now locked in a near fatal embrace,
as they ride the many hills of pleasure
and become a mass of whirling colour and sound.
In time the van comes to a stop,
the road quietens and they rest,
until the longing beckons them again.

Peter Maguire

The Wounded Soldier

He sat on the 'Baptist' wall
His blue uniform screamed out
His clean white shirt and scarlet tie
His stick, his piecing eye.
She saw him many yards away
Excitement ran from head to toe,
He looked like Errol Flynn - a wounded Robin Hood
I think, I think he fancies me
Will he follow, will he talk, will he just say 'Hi?'

She drew level and he just got up
And took her hand in his and in
A Northern accent, said, 'Can I walk you home?'

She just squeezed his hand, her voice had disappeared.
She'd become a trembling wreck
Thinking never never let it end.
She said she'd see him once again
Tomorrow would be good -
But he arrived anxiously, too early
And from a bus, she stood - in front of him
In gym-slip, with satchel, hockey stick.
For she was just thirteen years
And he was twenty-two.

Joan Richardson

Self-Portrait

Crossing what must have been the park,
wearing, I believe, black high-heeled sandals
and a very short, shiny, summer dress,
my hair falling down my waist,
I wasn't considering appearances.
With my conqueror's soul I was marching
in the platinum brilliance of a noon
which also belonged to Alexander, to Caesar.
I was only afraid of sand, insignificance.

Then the voice of a stranger: 'Excuse me,
please allow me to say this:
you're the most beautiful woman I ever saw.'
I woke with a start.
But smiling, I replied with perfect ease,
every inch a lady: 'Thank you,
what a lovely compliment.'
He bowed and passed.

My unreal existence, all these
forced courageous marches through the world,
myself undaunted by ambushes, javelins, blizzards,
seasoned by decades of sieges and pitched battles,
disguised as a pretty woman.

Susanna Roxman

Foreplay

With working-folk, it's especially untrue:
When the expert, didactic, tells you
That blokes do all the chasing,
Especially in these grab-all days,
Just tell him politely, 'Shove it!' arseways.

Travelling, as you're prone to,
Through inevitable pubs, mark well
Those feted handbag-packs
Surrounding, teasing, reversing the role
That gives the strutting peacock his goal.

Usually, there's at least three of 'em,
This is a requisite minimum,
So if one gets to score,
The luckless won't be bored.

(Well, this is the age of consideration
According to the Charters scuttling the nation:
You can't afford to leave the packs out:
They're what gives any charter its clout)

As with any aspiring Military junta,
A well-drilled battleplan is the imperative order:
Spread out evenly, an orderly line,
Tip the old wink, the nod, the sign,

Fax the sly look round the teeming pub,
Chuck the signals like hand grenades into the hub,
Watch the explosion bring 'em running,
Tongues like parched alsatians: cunning.

The ritual then is simple, result the bitter part:
Tricks of an animal order seldom bring reward:
This doesn't mean to say that boys don't have their tricks:
That behaviour's obvious, the ritual in their pricks.

Tom Miller

Hip Tips for Hot Dates

OK, say you have a ticket
For the new Tom Stoppard play
'But I hear it's flawed . . . '
That's not the point says Mae.

Who knows about these things for sure
(She once had phone sex
With the sound guy from The Cure).

No, better yet, send him a book
Prove your intellect
'Joanna Trollope?'
Oh, don't be wet -
Greil Marcus or Martin Amis
He's a *man* don't forget.

Make sure you don't act girlie
Match him glass for glass
And if he doesn't bite says Mae
Then he's probably underclass.

So it's row G for Arcadia
And triple tequila shots
Followed by tough discussion
Of Martin Amis' plots.

Yeah, he bites all right
Takes a large chunk from my purse
And after brief, blurry snogging
Says he's got a girlfriend, some nurse.

One day I'll call Mae
Just to thank her
Brilliant advice, but you forgot:
'Watch out for the wankers!'

Glenda Richards

Stay for the Ride

Say run, and go now.
Say stay and stay now.
Say go now and stay.
Say stay and go.
Say one thing and do another.
Say to another one thing.
Say to yourself another
and you will do another's thing.
What then is this thing?
The thing is the doing or not doing.
The thing is not the saying or the going it is the
staying for the ride.

Mireille Chan

Untitled

Apricot sun-kiss
Tomato skin-lips

The stars rearrange
  Themselves tonight,
    Nestled in warm sticky ear

The sand in your pockets
Fell into the dirty socks
At the bottom of my
Sleeping bag

And then,
        Into a letter,

Arriving in Paris in the morning,

To bring colour to my face

Again.

Christian de Nimes

Fever Pitch

A chemical frenzy engulfed me in haste
A glowing sensation that rose to my face
A hungry lust that I longed to feed
With raging passion he would fill this need

Proceed with the chase as I took to the floor
Homing in on the body I'd want all the more
The flashing lights and electric itch
Amassed my senses to fever pitch

I searched for a sign, he threw back a glance
Like a mesmerised child I was locked in a trance
Our bodies drew closer, pushed by the crowd
My voice was unheard, the music too loud

The smell of his body, and warmth of his skin
A blistering fire that was burning within
Moist tender lips that showered my face
Impatient arms entwined in embrace

Feeling the urgency, holding me tight
Leaving the club we sped into the night
Not knowing his name, not wanting to care
Just needing to fill this emotion we shared

Arrived at a park not a word had been said
In dark eerie silence to a bench I was led
Stars filled my head, and joy filled my heart
Fulfilling the lust that I'd felt from the start.

Rachel Bourne

A Man Stood in Front of His House With Rain Descending
(After David Hockney)

The Painter got it wrong - this is not my house at all,
although I've very English, it's really not my castle,
in fact, it is the fixed abode of the woman that I love,
in whose orisons my sins are all forgot:

She's never been at home to me, you see.

A lonesome cloud hangs over me
and slowly pours its heart out,
smudging my cracked cheeks,
my plaintive blue eye,
my crisp white shirt and crimson tie.

Meanwhile, the artist has very kindly taken time
to inscribe upon my hat a single, simple slight:
Idiot, in black.

Of course, I oblige and play the Fool
with a stiff-upper lip and porkpie hat
(the brim of which is full as a butt)

I hold my black umbrella out at arm's length
like a dangerous bird of prey, distressed
in case its carrion black might damage or defame,
(or perhaps profane and slightly strain) my dignity.

And my Love hides behind her battlements
and squeezes out her tears and I loiter here in vain,
wishing it was my house and I had the keys to get in
out of this outrageously persistent, localised rain.

Ed Prichard

The Spiralling of Winter Ghosts

The spiralling of winter ghosts
In and out the fog
Touching things not meant to feel
The frigid hand that's lost
Images vanish before the eye has seen
Flitting inside the head
Of the mind that is here
The other side of dead
Peace is unknown
To those that dwell elsewhere
A life that passed the boundary
And trapped the spirit in there
Trapped the life, now immovable
Caught as flies in aspic
Communication through flickering fancies
Held only when fate sometimes chances
Movement and invention are foreign alien things
Life without solidity
Is chaos inside
Greater but unseen rings
Walls of fog surround
Protecting non life's static stagnant whole
Rotting from internal self made wounds
Self-righteous, proven right to choose
Remain inside
Within your eggshell of ignorance
In a womb
Of certain clockwork doom

David Foster

Spermicidal Maniacs

5 . . . 4 . . . 3 . . . 2 . . . 1 . ∴
They're off
Bombing alone the inside lane
Giving it some wellie
Two spermicidal maniacs
Riding the same rocket
Down the same tube
0 to 60 in no time at all

Out from one
Into another
Sod off you bastards
We were here first
Keep your eyes peeled
For that left turning
A little short cut

Two spermicidal maniacs
Riding the same rocket
Now spy the egg moon
Full speed ahead
We wanna be first

Dive on in
Get well in there
Dig deep
We want it to be twins.

King Brian Boru

Loving or Loved

Be kind and care,
And I'll abuse,
And the nice'll be nothing.

Be cool and unfair,
And I'd sell my soul
For a 'drop o' the milk'
To drown to death in.

You like to think I don't care.
I like to think that you do.

Social games,
The only 'where it's at'.

So give it a cat,
To scratch and bite,
Turn out the light
And scream aloud.
Not too hard,
Not too nice,
'The Japanese use rice'.
Gimme a louse
Every once in a whine.

Belinda Baily

The Smoke Tower

Standing proud and dominant,
a landscape marred with smoke,
Sun temporarily appearing behind its shadow.
Disappearing as quickly as it came.
Buildings intervene, as human,
distorting the image,
seizing the apparel.
Its owner of desirous lure,
yet receiver netting in essence
but its function and sight.
Does it stand alone,
surrounded by a few scattered remnants,
or will it as a whole
reveal its wish
Be it as indifference, weakness, relish or love.
To tumble brick by brick,
a fragmented sketch of life.

Kate Lewis

I See a Future you See a Candle

Sitting there quietly afterwards,
You place a hand on your chest
To measure the dying beats
And slow yourself for rest.

I'm anxious, excited, moved by
The beauty of it all and trying not to squirm
I poke you on the nose
Tickle your side
Make clown faces . . .

You're silent, still, left
Staring at the candle
Watching the purple wax
Bead, drip, freeze.

I play with your hair
Run a finger along your ear
Kiss your back . . .

But you keep staring
Still clutching your chest
You pass me the mineral water
Then lie down and turn your back.

I remain thinking for a moment,
Swallow, then do the same.

Todd Mortensen

Woman

The female mind, it is so hard to explain,
it can cause a man unending pain;
unpredictable in the way it acts,
when we are accused of lacking tact.

The long flowing hair caressing your back,
timeless eternity grooming it, such a visual it packs;
your slender body so vulnerable and slight,
Yet within patience and strength to match any might.

Your chest, your waist, your hips look so fine,
these curves bring countless offers you must decline;
you have so much to give with your tender love,
so pure and free as a flight fancy dove.

Not as physically strong, yet equal in part,
your soul entwining my whole heart;
legs look so sexual and long,
wrapped around me making love bond us strong.

So long is spent in the mirror for you to prepare,
you add your touches with unlimiting care;
the eyes, the lips, the cheekbones, even fingernails,
to please and tease the adoring males.

Your final appearance can look so stunning,
you choose your clothes with all your cunning;
the shortest, tightest fits to hug your figure,
even dresses with daring splits to send men wild with vigour.

Yet for all this you do to send men mad,
you're the one thing that can make them so glad;
and when you catch him and make him love,
you can send his soul to the Heaven's above.

Sean Cadwallader

Going Down

It would be bliss
to kiss
the small
confined mound
of dark
coloured hair
beneath
your briefest
of briefs

Yes

It would be bliss
if I could
kiss
you

there

Rael

West Bay Love Song

When I gave you my love
It was a silent act
cushioned by night, and
pierced by the sound of the bullfrogs
calling their loves
after the rain had gone.
You gathered me whole, plucked cleanly,
and lost yourself in the only mystery -
woman.

So I, being woman, foolishly
believed you were mine.
Now we sit in our silences
each in an individual pool.
There are no right words
to fill a silence like ours.

Now, when the rain falls
only my ears listen
the pillow comforts my fright
and the offspring of those
long ago frogs
croak under my window
the music of night.

Now the smell that was you
that permeated all my nights,
forgets to linger.
And when we meet,
we never bridge the chasm
isolation.
And we break down into this silence
this silence
that goes deeper
than any act of love.

And I am faced at last
with the only mystery.
What does our silence say,
our voice could not?

Maureen Roberts

Being Celibate

I am a single man
Living in the City.
During the day
I go about my tasks,
But what my thoughts are
You dare not ask.

And during the evening
It is very much the same,
My thoughts I'm afraid
Stay with me
And remain.

So when I go to bed
The familiar feelings,
Those 'well, you know' ones
Follow me
Inside my head.

And in the morning
I wake up
With *Kiss FM*
Beside me.
I turn over and say;
'At 6.30 in the morning
you have got to be
fucking joking!'

John Deverson

Militant

All those nights
We shared in bed
I knew our love
Was surely dead
Because you
Were always blue
And I
Was a Red!

Claire Newbury

Covetousness

wanting it as more than
it is for you my
eyes followed you all
night without always
knowing you smoked like
it was an essential part of the
conversation we're at the
door and I let my arm crawl
around your shoulders and pull me
to you and gave back words with your
cigarette pulled my bare
neck to kiss my cheek as if
you did it everyday but
striking sparks behind my
calm demeanour and I
didn't know you owned a
tie

Jennifer Chamberlain

Prey

I can't get up today
I'm scarce with all the pain
So lovesick that I could die
Your supple words have left me dry.

Why don't you take a sword
And drive it in my chest
And cut away my heart
And mutilate my breast
Drop fire on my flesh
Or nail me to the door
Cut off my empty arms
I'll only want you more.

I'll lie upon your table
Get naked,
Don't you see?
My hip, so wide and tender
My stomach round for thee
I offer precious blood
My mind upon the altar
My body a docile lamb
Desirous of my slaughter.

When you smile
I'm blazing
When you talk
I'm bright
So steal away my breathing
If you can't take my life.

Jacqueline M Rice

Song of Sharon

When we was down 'The Orchard Tree'
This geezer got the hots for me.
He moved in close, know what I mean?
I said, 'Get lost, you old has been.'

He asked me if I'd like to dance.
'Nah, clear off matey, not a chance.'
He'd buy a drink. 'What would I like?'
I glared at him. 'Get on your bike.'

We'd go up West then. Sod the cost.
I told him straight, I said, 'Get lost.'
He looked at me, his face downcast.
He'd got the message then, at last.

I ask you, what do blokes expect?
A girl like me deserves respect.

Rosemary Fisher

The Drought Club

When will it rain
On The Drought Club?
With whom can they curl?
Remember their mothers
Covet breasts
Join hands with
Blossom!
Crumple like dead butterfly wings
Lie close to the spirits.

When will the rain
Wet their dryness?
With whom can they flirt?
Dress dandy -
And open
Assert disbeliefs
Hesitate!
Just for one second before
They explode like sycamores into the wind

Emma Foulger

Thief

you're a lover determined to love but naive to the process
you take your drug when you want your drug
you push my face to your crotch
maid and martyr
I work away till my mouth fills with your fill
I'm not even given the satisfaction of a sigh
you're off the bed and out the door even quicker than it takes to peck
                                                              me on the cheek
you're a thief
you'd take more if you could
but your ego can't stand the fact that you don't satisfy me
so rather than attempt to take something you know you can't
you concede to your failing
it's all rather pathetic

furthermore
you slip your hand ever-so-gently
into my wallet
I catch you at it
yet another thief in the house of love
oh anais
I pray for a spy

and love's a million miles away
with another

Yvette Peden

You and me?

I try to be the same with you as I
would anyone else,
But I cant.
With you I laugh more.
I blush more easily.
I undress you with my eyes.
I'm funnier.
I feel you undress me with your eyes.
My heart beats so much faster when you're there.
We can talk for hours.

But you already have a girlfriend
of three years.
Why torment me so, and wear me down,
You and me can never be?

Ida Belso

Strength Will Prevail

My life is one I want to spend with you.
But you don't feel the same way that I do.
I've come to terms with the way that you feel.
It took a while but as you know time heals.
Through your choice a future with you is not to be.
Through that choice it has to be another man with me.

So don't disrupt my happiness 'cos you're no longer of interest.
I accept that you don't want me so accept that means I'm free.

I will continue with my life, forget you and ignore the strife
you caused me. You're my past. My strength's regained at last.

I venture out now seeing who I please.
From nowhere up you pop and disagree.
You try your best to dissuade me from him.
So my existence will be dull and grim.
You're jealous and you're angry when I'm with another.
Remember *you* chose *not* to be my lover.

Your attitude I won't stand for 'cos I've no intentions of a war
of words. You dealt the cards and to face that fact it's hard.

You can't abide me with someone so I'd say that you're the dumb
one.
For wanting me yet leaving me, forbidding anyone I see.

I was prepared to spend my life with you
And found you didn't feel the same way too.
I thank God that I missed what might've been.
I've viewed a side of you I'd never seen.
You didn't want commitment so you told me where to go.
The shoe's now on the other foot and kicking hard you know.

So don't disrupt my happiness cos you're no longer of interest.
I accept that you don't want me so accept that means I'm free.

I will continue with my life, forget you and ignore the strife you caused me. You're my past. My strength's regained at last.

Tessa Mondesir

From Smile to Satisfaction

Drawn towards your soulful eyes, I wondered what they saw
My heart it skipped, my stomach fluttered, I knew I wanted more.
Thoughts flowed fast, my mind ran freely, searching for the perfect
                                                                         ploy
Should I play the carefree spirit or perhaps, instead, be shy and coy.
I smiled a lot, as we engaged, in social chat and witty talking
With flirting eyes and body language, I set about the art of stalking.
I knew in you, I saw a form that I would like to have, to hold
So I spoke to you in innuendoes and hoped my stance was not too
                                                                         bold.
We never really mentioned sex, though touched upon its raw
                                                                    attraction
But deep inside I somehow knew that this would lead to satisfaction.
And then we started on the road, to laying down, to getting close
Until at last we made the moves and you, to the occasion, rose.
I remember how you pulled me near and spoke to me in caring tones
How we kissed and how you stroked, how we stifled throaty groans.
Your face took on a different form, whilst I just watched, elated
Your eyes were closed, your mouth part open and now and then you
                                                                     hesitated.
I'd never seen your arms so strong, I never thought you'd lift me high
So when you did I had to scream - I didn't feel it right to sigh.
Our limbs became entwined like snakes; that was where the chasing
                                                                         ceased
Where we both won, where we both dined, where we enjoyed a
                                                                    hearty feast.

Linda J Romain

In Winter

All too briefly, I think -
this is not the way it should be -
as you take me in, envelop me;
eager to receive
whatever meagre potion
I will allow.
Not hallowed perhaps,
but always the absolution
after the needing
after the sweat
the indiscretion of your pleading
for pearls of wisdom
not to be bestowed.
Afterwards, as we entwine,
I am stalking sleep;
anxious to avoid
the silence in your hands,
the weight of our bodies
upon the mattress.

In a dream
I'm loping through
flurries of new snow
all teeth and fur
under a bone-moon sky.
Running from the fire in you.
Running from the fire.

Vincent Woodcock

A Glance to Love

A glance that meets across a crowd filled space
    Not once, but twice - or even more
Until that glance is locked firmly in place
    Gradually a smile to draw.

Then purposely moving, close together,
    To a common place where one might
Ecstatically talk, and wonder whether
    They're making an impression right.

And then with a drink, and some sustenance
    The atmosphere will relax;
And if there is music, maybe a dance
    Would help a friendship then to wax.

The test of all this will then much depend
    Upon further meetings, where love
Is eventually declared the end
    Of fleeting glance o'er crowd above.

Carol Clegg

NB

Straights are major, gays are minor,
Transsexuals bitonal,
And awkward in their whole-tone
Scale some choose to be alone.

Aidan Baker

Wet Dream

The water was electric blue.
The sunlight stroking the eerie rocks all around them.
They moved like creatures from another age
Big white bubbles smiling
Slowly drifting along inside the huge glass box,
Floating horizontally, hanging upside down, never
ever breaking the smooth choreography of their strange soundless
                                                                                              dance
My finger caressed the window, unconsciously.
I swear he winked at me.
He came and stared, grinning and just kept close to me.
My fingers followed the contours of his lips,
Imagined touching his skin.
He was still staring.
I lowered my eyes, embarrassed.
A big blue world of silent beauty.
My heart suspended inside it.
Then a voice behind me:
'Maan . . . that whale really digs that chick . . . !'

Pascale Presumey

Kodak

Maybe he saw her in a crowd,
Just a face in passing.
But
now he thinks of her,
He wonders about her.
She has become
an itch
on his back
that can't be
scratched.

S Dass

From a Princess to Her King

First you showered me with stardust,
that late springtime in the early evening air;
Enticed me with your open arms,
Tied moonbeams to my hair.
Caught all my falling teardrops
in your enchanted lake;
Bewitched, they now are oyster pearls
Transformed for your keepsake.
I know you took them sailing,
Seeking pure silken thread
to tie those pearls to the jewelled crown
You will place upon my head.

Honor Crellin

Disciple

She loved the bearded guy on sight
and recognised he was a man apart.
He sat alone in the opening seminar,
El Greco faced, and never spoke
but his sad eyes wandered.

She waited for the break to pounce,
and they walked together in the garden.
His name was John; he came from Santa Fe;
his plump thighs strained his jeans;
he cracked bad jokes. Catastrophe!

Too late, she glimpsed the other one -
tall and lithe as a northern pine,
but pursued by the blonde from Illinois!
As John began to kiss her by the lake,
she dreamed of another bearded chin . . .

All week she worshipped from afar.
On the final day she shadowed him
to a store, where he tried out pens
with a slender, nodding wrist. He left.
She gazed in wonder at the scribble pad.

Seamus *Christie* Donovan! Holy name!
As if at school doing lines, she traced
his calligraphic form again and again
but with the soaring curves and flourishes
of love. She lost all track of time.

John's stubby fingers drummed the bar;
a bottle of wine was nearly empty.
'Christ woman! What's kept you?'
'I was paying my last respects,' she said
and poured herself a glass of blood.

Felicity Napier

In the Secret Garden of my Heart

Should I compare thee to a rose
Enigmatic in midst of bloom
Breathing soft perfume into the breeze which
of my heart fills every room.

Delicate pastel shades of every hue
Soft make-up of a female face
Which captivates each blinded eye
and fills with joy each barren place.

Should I liken your thorns to arrows of love
which spear my heart
why such pain from such great beauty
How can such love inflict such hate?
You are the cup on which I feed
though blow by blow you drain my soul
my broken heart to bleed.

Should I reap the seed you sow
I am the plant of love you grow
You are the water that I drink
Your scent the very air I breathe
Your love the light of life I see
The greatest love there is to me.

But like the rose of love and hate
Whose blooms fade and decay
broken hearts, forgotten hope
will turn to dust and float away
like petals in the final breeze.

Michael A Hurd

Maximes

Peculiar chance,
A casual glance,
Tonight won't be the same.

He meets your eye,
The tension is high,
It's all part of the game.

One small remark,
Now that bright spark,
Flickers into a flame.

You want to so much,
Just someone to touch,
Who cares about his name.

In for the kill,
Seeking a thrill,
And no one gets the blame.

Paula Brown

Combing

Young lovers on the beach
Combing through each others hearts and minds
Like beachcombers looking for loose change
Looking for the tides of each others moods
And the truth of each others feelings.
But as young lovers will do,
They lie on the beach
Corrupting the truth and the flesh of youth.
Hands outstretched and intertwined
In duplication of the driftwood.
Salt tang and musk
Drift them towards a new wave
Of sand soft and silent sweetness.
Skin, cobweb soft, on silken sand,
Stroking skin. Hands
Stroking long, silky soft sand coloured hair.
The strokes are swift, and peak
Like the incoming tide, which will soon ebb.
Hands and hearts disentwine
And the two lying on the beach
Realise the truth of the lie;
And, disengaged, comb with quiet attention
Each others face and hair free of sand.
Finished, they walk back up the beach
And when the driftwood is within reach
They can merely stare at what seemed to be
The truth, but was only a great lay.

Linda E A Hudson-Cooper

When Men Love

The Eskimo when courting an igloo he will make,
Take Harpoon, go fishing, to catch his wedding cake.
The Scotsman to the bagpipes, in a tartan kilt will twirl,
Prance and shout out, 'Scots W'hae,' impressing Scots girl.
The Irishmen we all know, have kissed the Blarney Stone,
They lead the maids a proper dance before they set up home.
The Englishmen will weigh things up, before they start romance.
They must be very, very sure, to luck they will not chance.
The Frenchman says, 'Oui Madame,' to Paris we shall go,
He knows just what the lady likes, and he will tell her so.
A Swiss will give you love on skiis up on the Matterhorn,
The German will be most precise, as to the manner born.
In Russia where it's very cold, you cuddle up in furs,
In China it's with Bamboo poles a man will win his spurs.
Americans have many ways uniting maid and man,
Cowboy ropes or Indian bows, are used within that land.
Australians are very tough as every Sheila knows,
He's boss in summer, and as well when the cold wind blows.
It does not matter whom you are, or where on earth you live,
Preparing life for married bliss, you have to take and give.
We all court in different ways, to show folk how we love,
The end result is just the same, two happy turtle doves.

Barbara Goode

What Durham Should Have Thought

The absence of sound
was obvious.
She had squeezed off
one bangle from her wrist.
There had been two.
They had been on her wrist for years.
Silence now allowed her
to move unheard.
One silver bangle
banging against the space
another silver bangle had occupied.
'You've taken off one of your bangles,'
Durham said
'Now I cannot hear
you moving around.'
He should have thought then
that something was amiss.

Andy Goldie

Thieves

All night the tense ticking of your clock,
A stray, unwanted touch of skin. A foot.
A sad excursion of some separate thought
Lost in limitless, undiluted dark.
Insensate sex. Familiar. Tiresome.
We turn our backs and wait for day to come.

Late afternoon. A pallid sun retreats
Behind a grouped reshuffling of cloud.
(Not quite the season for a barbeque.)
The first arrivals set out party-treats -
A hurried hoard of wine, some beer, a few
Dishevelled snacks. By eight we have a crowd

And all that being dulled by drink entails:
A random couple share a garlic dip,
Whilst others, drawn like moths towards the fire,
Congratulate the 'chef' - his choice of ales,
Reflect it hasn't rained, then disappear.
We move past midnight, never losing grip,

Until alone again. Your room is dead.
It rattles the rant of the departed.
Our shadows stand as if cut from a shroud.
We do not speak; we dare not touch. Instead
We sleep as thieves; alert, afraid, too proud
To return what neither of us started.

David Whatley

American in London

My mind had started
Racing long before
she took me in.
A glance across
The table the game of love
Begins.
We danced around the courtyard
Of course she led the way.
A subtle invitation a hint
That she would play.
Are you bold enough to take
Me was the message in
Her stride, a tantalising
Filly who was ready for
The ride.
Let me groom your supple
Body. Let me stroke your
Golden mane. Let me discipline
With firmness giving pleasure
Over pain. She was willing
She was able and she put me
To the test, an American in
London, she simply was the best.

Mark Tracey Dearan

Sonnet

I've seen the ads and now I'm going to do
Exactly what they tell me - they know best.
I'll sail the seven seas to get to you,
I'll climb the mountains and do all the rest.
And when I get down on one bended knee,
Throbbing with the passion that I feel,
At last I know that this will make you see
That I'm the one for you. I will reveal
My inner self, and then I'll take your 'and,
And you'll look up at me and then you'll sigh,
And tell me that you knew I'd understand,
And then you'll get your 'anky out and cry.
But if you still refuse to let me in,
This box of milk tray's going in the bin.

Lucy Wallace

Trojan?

Should he come to steal me today
As he stole me back then,
Would I go?
Hearing the years of screaming again?
Tasting the roasting flesh of men?
Knowing where it will lead?
But if he loves me and I love him . . .
Is love to be pursued beyond the suffering?
Beyond the pain we brought, we'd bring?
Why from such a charming, sparkling Gem
Should trouble like an army charge?
And why before all my own
The one I love is him?
I deceive and trick at every turn;
I smile with her and hide a jealous burn.
What fire, what destruction would we cause
Should desire ever overcome applause?

Helen Dunton

Just so Susie

Her furniture was Hi-Tec,
Silver knobs on matt black.

Fashion Designer (very successful),
Swimwear (exotic colours)
Rome, New York . . . all that.

And I swear that even Sherlock,
With his famous magnifying glass,
Would fail to find one blemish,
One spot, throughout
her entire flat.

We were workmen on the scaffolding,
who she may have found
'quite interesting.'

She passed us cups of tea
through the kitchen window -
Of another world she told us:
Jet Set, High Flying,
and let us choose between Assam
and the very best Darjeeling:

'Is that all right?'
'A drop more milk?'

And once when she wasn't there, we saw,
Laid out, in perfect order,
A complete set of underclothes
in the finest peach -
coloured silk.

Tony Maude

No Answers No Lies

She jokes,
'Who was he with last night?'
But I don't laugh.
She wants a confidante,
A friend in a storm,
But I'm on the other side,
Lying silently on the raft
She clings to.
I don't laugh,
Who were you with last night?
I cry
But I don't show her,
Or she'll know you weren't with me last night.
I don't laugh,
I don't answer,
I just look inside my head.
Then she says,
'Why is she better than me?'
Why is she better than me?
You think the questions end when I go home
Because I'm too scared to ask them.
I don't laugh,
You don't answer.
But truth is in silence,
Because silence cannot lie.
She cries,
'If you don't answer, what does that mean?'
I laugh.

Meryl O'Rourke

Party Victims

Women watch women, measuring like stoats,
- Carefully cautious of young Unattached
Who's wary as a rabbit of swift teeth upon her downy neck!

The crowded room - and dainty words from waxen lips,
Those who've captured, those who think they might -
And need to make provision for themselves, and theirs'
- A secret fight!

Avoid the shelf!
And so avoid the second choice,
Thick-fingered lifting down,
As though an ornament.

Such pretty predators these!
With victims scarcely knowing the score, or even why.
- 'I saw you talk to Mary-Jane!'
- 'Was that her name? - That funny, ugly little thing?
And such a mouse!'

Eyes widen like a cat's,
Cloud all-consuming terror of being left,
- Such longing to curl-up and rest!
Those pupils darken, chasing sky,
- So watchful now, they'd catch the merest straightening of a tie!

Virley Trezise

No Impediment

When formless thoughts entwine in secret worlds
When every longing, dream and thought are one.
When dawn and dusk alike drown deep in loving
And one beloved touch awakes the sun.
No music peals when that one voice is silent
Each hour apart a barren, empty waste
Till melding minds and bodies end the waiting,
Entwined, restored, one perfect whole replaced.
Ah that alone can truly be called 'Mating'.

Caro Manning Jeffrey

Meat Market Mating

Leering around the Singles Bar
A dim dear dive where desperation dwells
Falsetto giggles preceding 'come-on' smirks
From sleazy smears of smudgy lipsticked mouths.

A questing eyebrow quirks its sordid foreplay
Until it meets a pseudo-bored 'OK'
From easiest, sleaziest stalely lonely seeker.
Eager with feigned indifference they cross the room to meet.

Is this the dreamed-of long awaited Romance
Prelude to love Divine - or rutting swine?
Their coupling is one-up on masturbation,
No way real Mating - merely copulation.

Constance Jeffrey

The Love Game

She stared at me and fluttered her eyebrows,
I was sexually attracted to her, it had to happen now,
Then she was all over me, arms wrapped around my neck,
Pressed her lips heavily against mine, started to undress me -
'It'll only take a sec.'

She unbuttoned my shirt unexpectedly,
Just like I've seen on my TV.
She forced her fingers within mine,
(I knew this for her wasn't the first time).

She took the ring off my finger,
Fragments of the past she didn't want to linger,
My shirt wide open she gave me a long precious kiss,
I tried to kiss her back, but unfortunately it was a 'bad miss'.

She said, 'Gosh aren't you bony, you've got knobbly knees,'
She laughed when I told her I was afraid of bees,
She said, 'You've got a spot growing on your nose,'
Then I accidentally stood on her sore toe,
(Which was beautifully covered by a plaster),
This whole love game I couldn't master.

I wish she hadn't gazed into my eyes,
And gone on to tell me all those lies,
I didn't know she was one of my wife's spies,
The love game can be a person's demise!

John Gregory

Culmination

Your hand on my hip
Possessive, warm,
In control.
My desperation showing through
In kisses
Taut and pleading -
For contact,
A penetration to the core
Of hurt.
A unit of acknowledgement,
At least.

Your hand on my hip
Expert, routine.
Complacent now.

You smoke alone upstairs
While I
Wring out a desperate tear
And dress in the dark.

Eileen O'Donovan

Chopping Myself up

Do I trust you?
How much? This much?
Which bit of me do you want?

Do you want me?
Which bit? This bit?
How much of it can you take?

Do you have me?
Why me? Which me?
Did you notice when I put it there?

Is it safe

Am I safe

With you?

Petra Fried

Green Fingers

I suppose as they say
The sun will go on shining
The grass will go on growing,
If you go.
Who knows?
I know the sun will shine
But soft grass grow?
Under our tree,
You and her, laughing, joking,
Oh no!
Not if one girl
Went to mow.

Lindsay Maynes

A Love Match

Sublimation in the
sports court,
both of us thinking
that court was
so apt.

The party's quiet room,
the park,
the taxi,
my sofa . . .
both our minds racing,
tension building . . .
Do it.
Touch.
Kiss.
But what if . . . ?

We made it through
the minefield,
now I bathe
in the full beam
of your gaze.
Bliss.
You say this is
brilliant
and I must agree
it is.
It shines.
It is sublime.

Barbara Courtenay

Snakes and Ladders

Double six
I get to move.
Will she approve?
Oh! Bloody hell
she's coming closer,
Quick, up the ladder,
Pass the dice,
Oh! God, help me
she brushed my thigh!
'I'd better go and make some tea.'

'You're on my snake!'
I blurt out quick.
Oh! God she thought I meant my . . .
She giggles and then
stares into my eyes.
I've turned bright red.
This isn't nice
I haven't even got the dice.
'Make your move'
Hands on my knees
'Oh! please, Oh! please.'

'Come up my ladder, into my bed!'
'Claim your prize!'
I'm bloody sure that's what she said.
I wouldn't mind
But, oh! the shame
I never even won the game!
I'll be a man,
Be brave and mean.
Oh! I hope my underpants are clean!

Lloyd William Whicker